IMPACT

impact

HOW I WENT BEHIND ENEMY LINES IN OUR STRUGGLE AGAINST THE FAR LEFT

CASSANDRA SPENCER

HOUNDSTOOTH
PRESS

IMPACT

How I Went behind Enemy Lines in Our Struggle against the Far Left

ISBN 978-1-5445-1850-3 *Hardcover*

      978-1-5445-1849-7 *Paperback*

      978-1-5445-1848-0 *Ebook*

To my daughter, Lexi, who gave me the strength to keep fighting.

May you always be brave and true.

Contents

Prologue

I STOOD STARING OUT A WINDOW OF AN EL PASO hotel suite. The day was November 1, 2018.

"Are you okay?" James O'Keefe asked me. I had just finished my first story as a Project Veritas journalist—an investigation into the Beto O'Rourke Senate campaign in Texas.

"Oh, I'm fine," I said, somewhat unconvincingly, snapping out of my trance.

"We've given Corgi PTSD!" James joked, and the team who was there with us laughed.

Every time I think about that moment in late 2018, I smile and shake my head.

A lot of things happened that led me to that hotel suite... to being an undercover journalist...to being called Corgi and later Foxtrot.

Staring out that hotel window was surreal.

CHAPTER 1

A Justice Complex

I WAS ALWAYS AN ODD KID. MY TEACHERS IN ELEmentary school said I was ten going on twenty-five. During recess, instead of playing on the playground, I preferred to sit and read.

I came from a wealthy family in Hawaii. My father, Doug, was Honolulu's second largest personal injury attorney during the "glory days" of ambulance chasing in the late '80s to early '90s. He was a self-made man from Kentucky and the middle child of five, which definitely showed. He always had to do more to try and outdo his siblings. He got married and had a son right out of high school but put himself through law school. He started his own firm after that because according to him, no law firm would hire him. He had a reputation for being a ruthless attorney, whose other area of practice was drunk driving defense.

My mother, Karen, was the second youngest out of eight and was the daughter of two schoolteachers. My grandfather was Chinese and served at Pearl Harbor but happened to be off the day of the infamous attack. My grandmother was Japanese, and her family had immigrated to work on a pineapple plantation. I didn't realize until I was much older how crazy it was that my Chinese grandfather and my Japanese grandmother got together during the World War II era. After their marriage, they both became the black sheep of their respective families, which in hindsight is perhaps where I got my rebellious spirit.

Karen was very much the stereotype of Asian American success during that era. She spent her days playing tennis and shopping, had a "success perm," and many formal dresses I used to say made her look like Cruella de Vil from 101 *Dalmatians*.

The mansion I grew up in boasted a private pool and tennis court as well as live-in help. My parents were Honolulu socialites and held frequent parties in our house, which was decked out with bright white carpets and black marble, the style of the time.

* * *

I got accepted into Punahou School, Barack Obama's alma mater and one of the top private schools for Honolulu's elite. (Ironically enough, Barack Obama's fifth grade teacher, Mr. Eldredge, was my fourth-grade teacher.) I loved it at Punahou. All the other kids came from similar backgrounds, and despite being painfully shy, I remember having many friends and always doing well in school.

Then my parents dropped a bombshell—we were moving to Maui at the end of fourth grade. I was going to have to leave all my friends behind and start over in a new school. And not just any school, a *public* school. I had never attended public school.

The move to Maui was really rough on me. It was in Maui I found that during recess, I preferred reading books to playing with the other kids on the playground. My favorites were Michael Crichton novels, especially *Jurassic Park* and its sequel, *The Lost World*.

In addition, the other children didn't come from homes with parents who were the who's who of Hawaii high society. I just found there was a certain apathy at the school in general.

One big difference between public school and private school was cafeteria duty. Each day, classes rotated to work in the cafeteria to serve food, help wash dishes, and so forth. I did it once or twice and *hated* it. Some kids enjoyed it because it gave them a chance to leave class, but I didn't want to leave class. I wanted to learn, and I was already bored because my private school had been so far ahead academically.

I didn't understand why I had to work in the cafeteria. They offered free/reduced lunch to some students, so why didn't they work in the cafeteria? I didn't even eat the cafeteria food because I thought it was gross, so I brought lunch from home. I didn't derive any benefits from the cafeteria, so why should I be forced to labor in it?

*　*　*

So one day, I just said no. I explained to my teacher my reasoning and I refused to go. I did this publicly, in front of the other students, and about twenty other children decided to join me in my refusal. Eventually, the threat of detention got the other students to go and complete their cafeteria duty rotation. However, as the ringleader (and the one who remained continually defiant), I was sent to the principal's office.

When my father joined me there, I explained my reasoning in a calm manner. There were my main contentions:

- I was in school to learn, not to work in the cafeteria, and cafeteria took away from class time.
- I understood that even though I did not receive free/

reduced lunch, the lunches were still somewhat state subsidized. However, I brought lunch from home every day and gained no benefit from the cafeteria. Therefore, I had no obligation to contribute to it.

Instead of being annoyed that he was called to the principal's office over the matter or telling me to do as I was told, my father's answer surprised me:

"My daughter has a point. I don't see why she should have to do cafeteria duty."

From then on, when the rest of my classmates would go to cafeteria duty, I would instead go to study hall.

Even at ten years old, the idea that I had the ability to speak truth to power, even to adults, stuck with me throughout the rest of my adolescence. During high school, I became a somewhat frequent contributor to the *Maui News* Letters to the Editor section. In particular, I wrote several letters criticizing Judge Joel August. Hawaii, unlike other states, had judges appointed and not elected. And as a one-party (essentially), democratically controlled state, this meant that most of the judges were extremely liberal. After being outraged by a ruling, I decided to speak my mind and send in a letter.

To my surprise, my letter was not only published, but

a few days later, two responses to my letter were also published, one in support and agreement with me, and another dismissing my opinion due to my age.

One day, that judge came to speak at my school, and I remember being excited thinking this would be my opportunity to confront him head-on. I can't remember exactly why he was there to speak to us, probably some sort of career day, but I politely sat as still as I could until the Q&A session.

I formulated the perfect question. I didn't want to be overly confrontational off the bat, so I simply asked why Hawaii's judges were appointed and not elected. He gave some sort of milquetoast answer, and I retorted:

"Do you think the people of Hawaii are too stupid to pick their own judges? Or are you worried that if they had the choice, you'd be out of a job?"

I was escorted out after that, but I knew I had left an impression not only on the judge but also on every person who was in attendance.

CHAPTER 2

New York University

MARCH 2004, NEW YORK CITY

I WAS EIGHTEEN WHEN I MOVED FROM MY HOME of Maui and enrolled as a freshman at New York University (NYU).

I arrived in 2004 during the peak of the Iraq War. A couple of days after I moved into my dormitory in the heart of New York City, I remember watching a quarter million protestors go by the window shouting their disapproval of the war. My mother was worried for my safety as 9/11 was still fresh in the minds of Americans—the Republican National Convention was being held in the city that year, and my mom was worried it would be the reason for another terrorist attack.

The world was changing, and so was my family. After a tumultuous twenty-year marriage, my parents were getting divorced. In some ways, it was a relief; the fighting and drama could finally stop. At least that's what I naively thought.

And I had bigger concerns at the time, such as the cute twenty-eight-year-old from the New Jersey National Guard I had gone on a date with.

A strange thing happened on that date. Anthony and I went to the Metropolitan Museum of Art, where I told him I originally wanted to be an actress, but I had reevaluated such a childish thought.

It was a silly attempt to seem more like an "adult" while I was on a date with someone who was ten years my senior. He told me that it was actually a shame I had given up on something I felt passionate about. The problem was, I hadn't felt passionate about acting. I liked it, I enjoyed my time doing theatre, but was I *passionate* about it? No.

Dating Anthony, however brief, opened my eyes to the reality of war and the people who went. My privileged upbringing had given me the idea that joining the military was something "other" people did. At the very least, it was just a place for my father to threaten and send my delinquent older and younger brothers to straighten them out.

Anthony showed me another side to that. He wasn't a delinquent with no other way out; he was smart and funny and cultured. And he was about to go to Iraq as part of Operation Iraqi Freedom III (OIF III).

One evening, we were eating at a nice restaurant somewhere in Princeton, New Jersey. When he told me he was a lieutenant, I ignorantly asked him, "Is that like a sergeant or something?"

The "are you that stupid" look on his face made me flush red with embarrassment. I quietly resolved in my mind that I would make more of an effort to learn more about the military and about the war so I wouldn't look like such a silly little girl in the future.

After that weekend, I sat in an NYU dining hall with my friends from the dorm who were talking about Chanel handbags and how it was sad that I didn't have one. But I couldn't stop thinking about earlier that day when an argument about the Iraq War erupted in one of my classes. I remember thinking how uneducated all of it sounded because not a single person in the room had ever *been* to Iraq. What were a bunch of ignorant, spoiled, rich teenagers going to do?

This galvanized my resolve to educate myself further on the topic.

I thought that talking to a recruiter would be a good place to start learning. I made the mistake of thinking a recruiter would be a good resource to educate myself about the military. A war was going on, so at the time, recruiters had to be as smooth as used car salesmen. My intention was to simply ask some questions for a freshman English paper I was writing on the military pay/rank structure. But before I knew it, I was taking the Armed Service Vocational Aptitude Battery (ASVAB), where I scored in the top 1 percent and was thinking of dropping out of school to become a counterintelligence agent.

"You won't have to deploy with that job," they told me. (Lie.)

"You can just go back to NYU after your contract and the Army will pay for it!" (Exaggeration, at best. Although the GI Bill is a great program, it would not have covered the more than $40,000 a year that NYU, a private university, cost.)

Originally when I went to college, I had dreams of maybe working in the music industry or going to law school. I was an undecided major, so I didn't have a clear direction in life yet. In that moment, I resolved that I wanted to join the Army. I was fully prepared to drop out of college and enlist, and during finals week, I submitted transfer papers to go to the University of Tennessee (UT) that fall.

I don't remember much about my time at UT, aside from being on the color guard and going to bartending school. My heart wasn't in college, so I basically stopped showing up to classes.

That fall break, I went home to Maui and called one of my best friends, Matthew Ryan Hanson, whom I called Matty. We'd been online friends since my early teenage years, despite living in different states growing up (more on him in Chapter 5). I called him to try and convince him to join me in the Reserves.

"Come on, dude, just join. It's only the Reserves, and then they'll pay for your college!" I told him as I paced back and forth next to my grandparents' pool in Maui.

"We can go together! It'll be fun! Besides, I know you don't want to be stuck working in a sandwich shop forever."

After a lot of back-and-forth, we both decided to join the Army Reserves as intelligence analysts. It just happened that Matty's recruiter was able to take him to the Military Entry Processing Station (MEPS) closest to him first. At this point, it was nearing the end of 2005 and I planned to take at least one semester off from college to allow me to attend basic training.

As anyone who has joined the military can tell you, MEPS is your first stop on actually enlisting into the military. It is where you take your ASVAB, go through the many physical examinations, and eventually swear in. Oftentimes, the closest MEPS can be hours from your home, so it requires an appointment in advance. Many recruiters will put potential future recruits in a hotel the night before so that they can be there first thing in the morning.

Matty went to MEPS first and called me afterward. "So, a recruiter at MEPS talked me into joining Active Duty as a medic. That just means I'll be in a hospital, right?"

I smacked my forehead. I forgot to warn him not to let the recruiters talk him into anything else. Well, there went that plan.

I still planned to enlist because I didn't want to go back to school, so I left Knoxville, Tennessee, at the end of the semester and began to drive to where my mother lived near Sacramento, California.

One day, during my cross-country road trip, I stopped to check my MySpace messages and saw that I had a message from a soldier at Schofield Barracks named Jason.

In 2005, there weren't things such as Tinder, so a lot of people would meet online through MySpace. Schofield Barracks was located on Oahu, Hawaii, and my location on MySpace was still listed as Kihei, Hawaii, even though I lived on the mainland.

He sent me a message saying hello, and I responded by telling him he might want to tighten his search radius since Kihei was on Maui, a different island than Oahu where he was located. He asked if I wanted to keep talking, and since I was driving down I-10 on my way to Los Angeles to visit a friend before I went up to my mom's, I said sure.

We met when he flew to California for a long weekend a few days later, and shortly thereafter, I decided to fly to Hawaii to see him. I never got on my return flight.

Like most teenager's plans, mine fell apart when I decided to marry Jason after knowing him for a couple of weeks. No, I am not joking. It was 2006, and I was frustrated. I didn't feel right in college, and I had always been lonely. I was flattered that anyone wanted to marry me at all.

Jason was a specialist in the Army. We got married without telling our parents, and the friends who knew about our plan told me I had lost my mind, including Matty. I slept in his barracks room and hid during the day to avoid detection at the base until we had enough money scraped up to afford a tiny apartment, which took about a month, until his Basic Allowance for Housing (BAH) kicked in. BAH is one of the reasons so many young soldiers get married, because it adds to their paychecks and allows them to move out of the barracks.

You would think being a teenage bride would have made me feel weird or out of place, but the practice of marrying young is fairly common in the military, especially among the enlisted soldiers who don't want to live in the barracks and crave some sense of stability.

I didn't feel out of place, mind you, but I knew I had made a horrible error in judgment, literally the day I got married.

We hired a witness and got married on a beach by a preacher whom we found in the yellow pages. We had some time to kill before our appointment, so we went to a Dairy Queen before we got married. After the ceremony, we ate at a TGI Fridays, where Jason had to sneak me sips of champagne at the table since at nineteen, I wasn't legally old enough to drink.

That night, they had a party in the barracks, and Jason got too drunk and passed out in his bed. I went outside to sit next to a soda machine and called one of my friends, crying because I realized I had just made a huge mistake.

Even so, I told myself that I was an adult and I was going to live with the consequences of my actions. So I resolved to stick it out.

Six months later, I got pregnant.

CHAPTER 3

Pregnancy

PREGNANCY WAS A WAKE-UP CALL FOR ME—AND I mean that in the most literal way possible. We were on vacation visiting Jason's family in Birmingham, Alabama, when I shot up in the middle of the night.

"Jason, wake up. I think I'm pregnant."

"What?"

"I think I'm pregnant. Let's go get a test."

"It's 2:00 a.m."

Needless to say, I won out, and we went to the local drugstore in the middle of the night to get a pregnancy test. When it came back negative, Jason was less than thrilled that I had woken him up and dragged him out of the house for nothing.

When we returned home to Hawaii a week later, without telling him, I decided to take another one of the tests in the box. It was unmistakably positive.

Jason and I weren't trying to get pregnant, but we weren't *not* trying either. I thought that the pregnancy would somehow thrust me into the mindset of being a young wife and mother and that I would be content living the "Army wife" life—couponing, going to Pampered Chef parties, and so on.

But I wasn't. I was still as much a misfit as I ever was. I was just now dealing with morning sickness and frequent fainting from low blood pressure.

It did, however, give me a sharp contrast between my old friends, who were either still in college or working, versus the other young Army wives who all seemed to have babies or were pregnant as well. During college, I had always felt like an outsider, like someone who didn't belong or fit in. However, I felt even more out of place with the other wives and homemakers because growing up, I had always been more career oriented.

Realizing there was another human growing inside of me,

one who would look up to me and later scrutinize all my life choices, made me sharply aware that the decisions I'd made up to that point were more impulsive than I'd like them to be.

I was going to be someone's role model, whether I liked it or not.

One of the first things I did while pregnant was I enrolled myself back in school and, for the first time, took college seriously. Going to a satellite campus of Hawaii Pacific University was a long way away from NYU where I had started college, but I was determined to succeed. I didn't want my daughter to grow up and make the same mistakes her mother had.

I say mistakes because there was never a period that I didn't know my marriage to Jason was a mistake. We were ill-suited for each other. He was from Georgia/Alabama and didn't have an ambitious bone in his body. I know this sounds harsh, but my friends and I often joke that he is the literal embodiment of Forrest Gump without the charm. Even Jason knew this to the point it was our joke, and in lieu of having a song like most couples, *Forrest Gump* was "our movie."

In 2007, when my daughter, Lexi, was born, the war in Iraq was still going strong. So strong, in fact, that there was a controversial policy in place known as stop loss. If you were scheduled for a deployment, even if your initial enlistment contract was scheduled to end, you would be involuntarily extended for the duration of deployment. Jason was affected by this policy, so we decided that I would move to Birmingham, Alabama, with Lexi. Once he got out of the Army, he would join us. Jason's parents lived in Birmingham, so this way, I would have help and support, since at that point in time, my mom was living in California and my dad in Idaho.

Since I wasn't working, I put all my effort into school, going to the gym to get myself back into shape after the pregnancy, and being the best mom and wife I could possibly be. While Jason was deployed, I took at least one picture of Lexi each day and emailed them to him so that he would feel like he was getting to watch our baby grow (as much as he could) from Iraq. I breastfed Lexi exclusively after reading studies that it was the "best" option, and when she did go to solid foods, I made all of her baby food myself.

Despite never having held a baby or changed a diaper prior to giving birth, I found loving my own daughter to be surprisingly easy. Especially during all the time we spent alone, she became my little buddy. My sidekick. And as she began to look more and more like me, she became my Mini Me.

Jason and I bought a house in Fultondale, Alabama, in a new neighborhood. I finished my associate's degree with a 3.8 GPA and started in the ROTC program at the University of Alabama at Birmingham (UAB) to finally fulfill my dream of becoming an Army Officer.

CHAPTER 4

My Messy Personal Life

IN 2008, I DIVORCED LEXI'S DAD. HE CHEATED ON me, while in Hawaii, after coming home. I acted like I was upset, but secretly, I was relieved to finally have an excuse to leave.

In 2010, I graduated college and commissioned as an Officer in the US Army Reserve. After college, I no longer had a reason to be in Alabama, especially since following our divorce, Jason decided to reenlist. Since he didn't live there either, I moved back to Hawaii.

My career got off to a promising start. Even though I was a reservist, I was assigned to a mixed active/reserve unit. I was the Public Affairs Officer for the 500th Military

Intelligence Brigade (500th MI BDE) and I loved what I did. Because the unit was mixed, there were a lot more opportunities to be on orders rather than the one weekend a month that most reservists work.

Although my career was off to a good start, my personal life continued to be, in a word, messy.

I should preface this with some background information about my family. Around the time I left for college, my younger brother, Thornton Spencer, struggled with drug addiction. His drug of choice was heroin. While I was attending college and raising Lexi in Alabama, my parents desperately tried to save their son. Thornton went to every kind of rehab imaginable but to no avail. He never got clean for any meaningful period of time.

During one particular incident while I was pregnant, my parents flew me out for a failed intervention that ended with Thornton pulling a knife on everyone before fleeing. My daughter, even before birth, was my top priority, so I decided after that incident that unless Thornton was clean, I wanted nothing to do with him. I didn't want to see him or talk to him. If he was going to be present at a family gathering, I refused to attend.

When I was getting ready to graduate college, my dad tried to convince me to move to Maui. He assured me repeatedly that he would not try to move my little brother back to Hawaii, because he knew I didn't want to be around him. I agreed.

Before commissioning in August 2010, I had to complete the Leadership Development and Assessment Course (LDAC). Since I was going to move back to Hawaii afterward, I had put my car on a boat to right before I began the month-long course. In addition, the Army knew to send me to my home of record, Hawaii, and not back to where my school was.

I commissioned at Fort Lewis, Washington, after completion of the LDAC, and my parents both flew in to attend the ceremony where, as luck would have it, Thornton was living relatively nearby. He was doing poorly. By then, he was homeless and living on the streets. It's not that no one would take him in, but the condition was, in exchange he had to get help for his addiction. He chose the streets.

I told my parents not to invite him to my commissioning ceremony. I was becoming an officer in the Army and I didn't want to bring my homeless junkie brother on post. Reluctantly, I did agree to have dinner with him, my dad, and my uncle the night after the ceremony. Thornton showed up approximately three hours late, clearly high, and in the photo my dad insisted we take, his ribcage was clearly visible. He looked emaciated from life on the streets.

That dinner took place on August 8, 2010. Ten days later, on August 18, which happened to be my twenty-fourth birthday, I celebrated alone in my dad's house while, after numerous missed flights and failed attempts to bring him to Maui, he and his wife drove to the airport to pick Thornton up.

Even though I lived in a separate cottage on the property and Thornton lived with my dad in the main house, his being around created a lot of conflict. One of the conditions of living at my dad's was no drinking or drugs, but that didn't stop Thornton from wanting to disrespect the rules. One day, he sent me a Facebook message asking me to buy him alcohol.

"What?" I responded. "Absolutely not. You know the rules. You have the option of telling our father that you asked me to buy you liquor, or I am going to."

Thornton threatened to "beat my ass," and I was even more done with him than I already was. Living next door was tense. There were frequent incidents where Thornton showed up high and trashed the house. Obviously, I didn't want Lexi to be around that behavior, but when I got mad and complained to my dad, he would scream that I was the cause of all the tension in the house.

When I was preparing to go to South Carolina for four months of orders, my father told me I'd need to find another place to live when I got back. I panicked because my job with the military was on and off. I would often work for a few weeks and then be off for an undetermined amount of time, so I quickly married the guy I had been dating at the time who was active duty at Schofield Barracks on Oahu. I saw it as an option to avoid homelessness and to get away from the drug den my father's house was becoming due to my brother's actions.

Like the first time I got married, I knew it wasn't a great decision. (My second husband was also named Jason, so we'll call him Jason Two.) He was getting ready to deploy to Afghanistan, and even though we had been dating, it was largely a marriage of convenience that most people in my life don't even know happened. Throughout our entire marriage, I was either away on the mainland on orders, or he was in Afghanistan. During the "marriage" (if you can even call it that), we actually spent *less than a month* living together. In total, our marriage lasted a little over a year, and it only lasted that long because we were never in the same place at the same time. As soon as we were both in Hawaii, we got divorced.

When I reluctantly admit to people that I've, in fact, been married three times, I often used the following phrase when describing my second marriage: "If you blinked, you missed it."

And yes, I married again.

In 2012, I met Derek. We married a little over a year after we met. This time, however, we married because we *wanted* to marry each other. I can confidently say that I did love Derek, and regardless of everything that happened, I have nothing negative to say about him. He was a farm-boy and football player from Montana and continues to work on submarines in the US Navy. Marrying him was the first time I felt like I had gotten marriage "right." We had a lot in common, but he also pushed me to expand my thoughts and values on the things we didn't have in common at first.

He was a major factor in why I shifted my position on the Second Amendment, for example. Growing up in Hawaii, guns weren't a "thing," so while I supported the Second Amendment in theory, in practice I didn't see what the fuss was all about.

During our marriage, he was part of a group called the Hawaii Defense Foundation, which promoted gun rights in a state with arguably the most restrictive firearm laws in the country. Derek and his friend Chris would frequently post on the Honolulu Police Department's (HPD's)

Facebook page with information about how if people in Hawaii could defend themselves easier, certain crimes could perhaps be prevented. They didn't post anything with foul language or anything that could be considered reprehensible, but the HPD deleted all their posts and eventually blocked them from the page.

Derek, Chris, and the Hawaii Defense Foundation sued, and eventually won on First Amendment grounds since the HPD was running an official government page, on government time, and therefore were obligated to have a social media comment policy that treated differing opinions as equal.

If life is, in fact, a story with a predetermined outcome, some might say the lawsuit against the HPD regarding censorship on Facebook foreshadowed events to come.

Out of respect for his privacy, I won't get into the details of my marriage to Derek, but we went through a lot together, including my getting into a bad car wreck that would eventually end my military career.

Our marriage was already under a great amount of external stress when Thornton lost his battle with drugs in March 2015, shortly after his twenty-fifth birthday.

Even as kids, Thornton and I were never particularly close,

and I hadn't had much contact with him in the years leading up to his death. I was sad but not surprised. I don't have any regrets about how I handled things because my priority was to protect my daughter. The people whom I actually felt the worst for were my parents because being a parent myself, I can't imagine the pain of losing a child, regardless of the circumstances.

A couple of months after that tragedy, Derek made the decision to end our marriage. I left Hawaii battered and bruised. Physically, I was still in constant pain from the car accident, and emotionally, I had been through a lot. I went to California and got a contract gig at Intel in Folsom. I begged Derek to reconsider and hoped to reconcile the marriage, partly out of love but also partly because I didn't want to live with the shame that I was barely thirty and would have three failed marriages under my belt.

My personal relationships were a mess, and my career was falling apart due to the car accident, but my friends had been, and continue to be, a solid source of strength for me for which I am eternally grateful.

CHAPTER 5

Matthew "Matty" Ryan Hanson

LIKE MANY TEENAGERS GROWING UP IN THE EARLY internet era, I came armed with a MySpace profile, an AOL Instant Messenger (AIM) account, and an online diary. Mine was through the website LiveJournal, and my friends and I religiously documented our daily lives. Looking at my early writings from those days, I was very clearly the target demographic for LiveJournal: an angry, angsty teenager who desperately sought validation from strangers on the internet.

I made new friends through the site, including one boy from Ohio named Matthew Ryan Hanson. Matty, as I later grew to call him, had an upbringing almost opposite to my own. He grew up lower middle class in Toledo, Ohio, and dropped out of high school after getting a woman, who was nearly ten years his senior, pregnant. Despite the massive differences, we bonded over our mutual interests in movies and books and talked about our dreams for the future.

We stayed online friends, and when we were both eighteen, we found ourselves both living in New York. He was upstate nearly five hours away, but one weekend, he decided to come down to the city for a rave. It would be the first time meeting each other in the flesh.

I got to the club and was worried I wouldn't be able to find him over the massive crowd and blaring techno music.

"CASSIE!" I heard from a distance. Matty ran toward me through the crowd and gave me the biggest hug, picking me up off the floor. There was not a beat of awkwardness between us, and we talked and danced the night away. He had to return home the next morning, so it was a short meeting, but we stayed in constant contact throughout our lives.

* * *

When I decided to leave NYU to join the Army, I didn't want to go alone. The idea of basic training was so far out of my element at the time that it terrified me. Hence,

I tried to get Matty to join me during fall break. His upbringing certainly didn't offer him the same opportunities I had, and I knew one of Matty's biggest goals was to "make something of himself." I told him joining the Reserves would be a great way for him to go to college and not worry about the price tag. His ambition to be better than what he was continued to be the driving factor through the rest of his life.

Like I mentioned earlier, we had a plan: we were both going to enlist into the Army Reserve as intelligence analysts. Matthew was never big on the idea of going to war and being on the front lines. He looked at the Army as a means to an end: to get him to where he wanted to go in life.

Matty became part of the 101st Airborne out of Fort Campbell, Kentucky. Matty and I were both always somewhat impulsive teenagers, and the day before his graduation from basic training, he married the girl he was dating, Sarah.

When Jason was deployed to Iraq and Lexi was a baby, I made a trip up to Kentucky with my father to visit my brother. We happened to go through Fort Campbell the day before Matty was set to deploy to Iraq himself, so we stopped by and he got to meet my daughter.

For the longest time, our friendship flowed that way. Every

few years, we'd see each other when life allowed our paths to cross. After we saw each other briefly before his first deployment to Iraq, it was another five years before we saw each other in person again.

Before my car accident in 2012, my unit sent me to get officially qualified as a Public Affairs Officer (even though I had been serving as one for over a year already). The Public Affairs Qualification Course (PAQC) was located at Fort Meade, Maryland.

* * *

While I was busy getting my career off the ground, Matty served two combat deployments and reenlisted to finally get the hospital job he had wanted when he first enlisted. He was an LPN at Walter Reed.

When we found out we were going to be in the same geographic area for the first time in our lives, we were both ecstatic and couldn't wait to hang out on a regular basis. When I flew into the Baltimore airport, I arrived in the middle of the night, bleary eyed from the long trip from Hawaii.

"CASSIE!" I heard from across the baggage claim. Matty came bounding toward me, picked me up, and gave me the best hug I've ever gotten in my entire life.

Some of my most treasured memories were during these months. Matty, by then a sergeant, and I, a first lieutenant, saw each other regularly and got to be "normal" friends, not just "internet" friends. The time together brought Matty and me closer than ever, and when he got out of the Army, he even stopped and stayed with Derek and me for a bit.

So when 2015 rolled around and my life was falling apart all around me, I was happy to have a friend like Matty. By that time, we had been friends for more than a decade.

Matty, at that point, was living in the Bay Area, trying to realize his dream of becoming an entrepreneur. He was in Oakland, and I was living near Sacramento, trying to pick up the pieces of my life. I was working on a contract as a communications specialist for a tech company, and we frequently talked about getting together but always made excuses. We were too busy, the drive was too far, and so forth.

One day, I called him while I was in the sandwich line of the cafeteria where I worked, and he tried to convince me to come up to the Bay Area for the weekend.

I didn't realize that would be the last time we ever spoke.

* * *

About a week and a half later, I was with my Army Reserve unit, doing the regular Reserve schedule of working one weekend a month in Vallejo, California. At the time, I was the acting commander of the unit since the commander was going through the same Public Affairs course I had taken in 2012. I was still in a tremendous amount of pain from the accident, but my job mainly consisted of office work, so that wasn't a problem. (However, I gained a tremendous amount of weight and got out of shape, which was becoming an increasing issue for a military career, which has strict standards for height and weight proportions.)

I was taking my soldiers out to lunch, as was the standard protocol, and was sitting in the passenger seat of a rental car while we drove to Subway, when I got a Facebook notification:

Sarah has tagged you in a post.

Shockingly, Matt's marriage to Sarah, at nineteen years old, didn't last either. I hadn't seen or talked to Sarah in years. I opened the Facebook app to see a picture of the four of us, Jason, Matty, Sarah, and me, from a trip to San Antonio years prior, shortly before I became pregnant with Lexi.

Then I looked at the comments and saw people sending

their condolences. I quickly messaged Sarah, and she called me to say Matty had been murdered. She didn't have any details but knew that some of his friends and associates in California had been trying to get ahold of me because they knew we were close.

Shocked at the news, I sat in that Subway, my appetite completely gone. *How was this even possible? Who would want to kill him? He was only thirty years old.* I sat alone since my soldiers knew I needed the space. I kept my composure during lunch, but when we left Subway and went back to the unit offices, I told the first sergeant to take over. "I'll be in my office, but don't bother me unless it's extremely urgent."

* * *

Alone in my office, I broke down and sobbed. One of my best friends and closest confidants was dead, and I was never going to see him again. No more huge running hugs. No more late-night conversations where we talked about big plans for our future. None of it.

Later that day, I spoke to Matty's business partners who had been trying to get ahold of me. They told me the murder happened a couple of days ago and that his killer, Gale Lee Boyd, died during a standoff with the police in Southern California. He shot himself in the head and was pronounced dead at the hospital. My initial reaction was anger. *Why did this happen?*

I dropped everything I was doing for the next week and helped arrange Matty's funeral.

Maty was shot in his home. He lived in a mixed work and living space in Oakland. A former business associate had come and gunned him down in the entryway to his home. The business relationship had fallen apart because, according to everyone I talked to, Lee was "psycho." It sounded like the motive for the murder surrounded a woman, Celeste, who was Lee's "assistant" and girlfriend. Even though he was married, he was having an affair with Celeste.

Matty was always one to play the hero, especially when it came to helping damsels in distress. So when Celeste called from Vegas to tell him Lee was abusive and that she was scared, Matty immediately went to fetch her and bring her to California.

According to official reports, at 9:25 a.m., Lee Boyd came by the mixed work and living space where Matty lived and used a cement block to smash a glass door. Lee demanded to see Celeste, and I believe Matty lied and said she wasn't there. Lee left, and Matty put Celeste into an Uber in a back alley so she could get away to safety.

Why Matty didn't leave as well, I'll never know.

* * *

About forty minutes later, Lee returned and shot Matty six times in the chest. A neighbor came by to try and administer first aid, but it was clear that Matty didn't have a chance.

Lee confessed to the murder to several people after fleeing the scene. He ended up in a several-hours-long standoff with the police who caught up with him in Southern California a couple of days after the murder. Lee shot himself in the head and died in the hospital the following day.

To this day, the facts of the case enrage me when I stop to think about them. Lee Boyd, a loser and a coward, took his own life and never had to face justice for the crimes he committed.

When I arrived at Matty's house, there were flowers on the ground to cover the bloodstains.

Matty had a rough childhood, so he was not close with his parents. He hadn't seen his son in years. The people who showed up to his house were an assortment of friends, an ex-girlfriend, a wife none of us knew he had (similar to *my* second marriage), and business partners. The only family Matty was close to was his grandmother, Meems, whom I clung to throughout the ordeal and maintain a close relationship with to this day.

Going through his belongings and seeing them get divvied up was strange. I was asked if there was anything I wanted to keep, and I said no. It just didn't feel right. Nothing about the situation was right. The whole thing was and continues to be surreal.

According to Matty's obituary:

> After he was honorably released from the Army in January of 2016, he moved to California to pursue his dreams of becoming an entrepreneur. He proceeded to touch the lives of every person he met and he believed in helping them reach their full potential; he could inspire a mouse to become a lion.
>
> Matthew had grand dreams and took great risks to achieve them. He was incredibly determined and had a flare for both the artistic and the dramatic. He was constantly evolving and improving both himself and those around him. His energy was contagious, and he was surely destined for great heights. Sadly, he was taken from our world too soon.

I gave a eulogy at Matty's funeral. I spoke about how everyone there should do their best to reach their full potential and make an impact on this world because that's the legacy Matty would want to leave.

I'm sure I sounded very brave when I spoke, but to be completely transparent, Matty's murder was what finally broke me. From 2015 to 2016, my younger brother died, my husband left me, and one of my best friends was murdered. I needed a fresh start.

At the end of that summer, I packed up all my belongings and moved to Austin, Texas. Did I have a job lined up? No. Did I know anyone in Austin? No. But I knew I hated everything where I was and that I wanted to leave. Lexi had spent a year at school in California, but I don't think either one of us really cared for life there. California was always meant to be a transition. Either Derek and I would reconcile and I'd move back to Hawaii, or I would move on to whatever the next chapter of my life was.

One of the only things I took refuge in during this time were video games. I had experience working in tech, and Austin seemed like a logical choice of where to move to further my career. It was also listed as a good city for young professionals, and now that I was divorced and no longer in the military, I was desperate to find a place where I felt I belonged.

Before we moved to Maui, my family actually almost

moved to Austin when I was ten, going so far as to buy a house in the area and tour the school I would have attended. Austin was on the shortlist of places where I had considered moving after NYU, but instead, I chose to go to Knoxville. Something about Texas had always resided in the back of my mind, so I decided to follow my heart and come here.

I was clearly suffering from post-traumatic stress after the events of 2015–2016, so when I decided to move to Texas that summer, my dad suggested I let Lexi stay with him and his wife, especially since I didn't have a job lined up because it would give me time to get on my feet. By this point, he lived in Virginia, and I agreed to his suggestion. I didn't think much of it since Lexi stayed with my dad without issue when I had to travel for the military.

Up until then, a lot of the mistakes I made in my life were pretty obvious. But as you'll see, none of them compared to trusting Doug Spencer. That ended up being the biggest mistake of my entire life.

CHAPTER 6

The DeploraBall

WHEN I MOVED TO TEXAS IN SEPTEMBER 2016, I was diagnosed with fairly severe PTSD that for a time included being agoraphobic. Any one of the events that had happened over the preceding eighteen months would have been enough to send someone into a mental health spiral, but Matty's death for me was the last straw. I didn't want to leave my house. I didn't want to be around people. Most of the time, I had things delivered, but when I did venture out to go someplace completely benign such as Walmart, I went at 2:00 a.m. and would wander the store with headphones on to look busy and block out the presence of everyone else.

I was also in a large amount of pain due to the car accident that required a total of eight back procedures. I did not vote in the 2016 election, not only because I hadn't changed my registration to Texas yet but also because I had a back procedure that day.

I did support Donald Trump's presidency after seeing him speak at one of his rallies in Sacramento I attended with my mother earlier that year. I donated to his campaign and had a signed Make America Great Again hat. I didn't start off as a supporter, but his patriotism and love for this country shone through, and after having politicians who were so delicate with their words all the time, there was something refreshing about Trump. I often joke that he is the embodiment of the Freudian concept of id. Just raw, unfiltered emotion and passion. Often aggressive. Focused on actions and less on ideas.

Admittedly, I did not take him seriously as a political candidate when I first heard about him running. Around the same time, there was an article talking about Barack Obama going on some Discovery reality show, which prompted me to post on Facebook, "Politicians trying to be reality stars and reality stars trying to be politicians... What is our world coming to?"

I had always identified as a Republican but had become somewhat disenfranchised since in the pre-Trump days, it seemed like the party was more concerned with arguing over social issues I found to be petty. Being a multiple-time divorcée, it seemed horrifically hypocritical to act like I had any right to say who did or didn't get married. I had also smoked marijuana before and didn't see what the fuss was about.

So going into 2016, I wasn't really behind any of the candidates. I watched the primaries play out mostly apathetically due to my depression.

We had heard so much about Donald Trump's outrageous campaign that my mom and I decided to go and see what all the fuss was about ourselves. We went to a hanger in the Sacramento airport, and I waited to hear all sorts of outrageous ideas since all the news media seemed to treat the campaign like a joke.

I'm sure that in the back of my mind, this was one of the moments where I realized that the media really was "fake news," but I wasn't aware of it at the time.

I listened to Mr. Trump speak, and I found myself agreeing with what he was saying. Nothing he said was outrageous or racist. He talked about the broken media, the lazy recovery of the economy, and border security. Rallies really were Trump's place to shine. He came across as affable and genuine. It was such a stark contrast to what I had heard about his rallies and the outrageous behavior of his supporters.

What *was* outrageous, however, was the reaction of the

protesters outside the event. Several people got in the faces of my Asian mother and me, and one of them even vandalized her car while we were inside. The fact that these mostly white protesters were attacking me and my minority mother really illustrated how false the narrative was. So we threw our support behind Donald Trump.

I won't lie, though; I didn't think he was going to win the election. Every poll had him losing. According to them, it was seemingly impossible for him to win.

So I spent Election Day 2016 mostly in surgery and then in recovery from the anesthesia that evening.

I woke up around 8:00 p.m. and checked the results. It seemed Donald Trump was outperforming expectations, but Hillary was going to be the next president.

I dozed in and out of consciousness, and I thought that the drugs I was on must have been really strong because as the night went on, the impossible seemed to be happening.

It appeared that Donald Trump was going to be elected the forty-fifth president of the United States. I couldn't believe it. Even though I had supported him, I was shocked because every projection had him losing.

During the time leading up to the election, I was watching a lot of YouTube since I was terrified to leave my own home. I basically experienced the world through my computer. I watched several different conservative influencers, including Milo Yiannopoulos and Steven Crowder, when one video popped up as a recommended next video—*HIDDEN CAM: University of Houston Facilitates "Emotional First Aid Kits" for Students.*

The video was created by a group called Project Veritas, founded by James O'Keefe. James had become famous nearly ten years earlier when he donned a pimp costume, presented his partner, Hannah Giles, as a prostitute, and went to the community organizing group ACORN to see if the workers would help him cover up what was clearly illegal activity. The videos instantly propelled James to fame and prominence, and despite Democrats controlling the Executive Branch under Obama, as well as the House and the Senate, the videos were damning enough to get the entire organization defunded.

I hadn't kept up with his career, so when I visited the website this time, it was an "Ohhhh, it's THAT guy" kind of moment.

The *Emotional First Aid Kits* video was the first Project Veritas video I can vividly recall. Something about that video spoke to me, and I ended up binge-watching all the videos on their channel that night. They ranged from serious allegations of misconduct to sillier videos, such as the one that had drawn me in initially.

James O'Keefe established Project Veritas in 2011 as a nonprofit journalism enterprise to continue his undercover reporting work. Today, Project Veritas investigates and exposes corruption, dishonesty, self-dealing, waste, fraud, and other misconduct, in both public and private institutions, to achieve a more ethical and transparent society.

It spoke to me, and I thought to myself, "This is someplace I think I'd like to work," so I looked at their open positions. They had one listed for a communications director which fit my Army Public Affairs experience. I knew getting the job would take me away from Texas, where I had just moved, but something told me to apply.

A couple of days later, a girl responded to my email, saying they wanted to interview me but that things would be delayed until after the election.

I was so excited at the prospect of having a job that I picked up a copy of James's book, *Breakthrough: Our Guerilla War to Expose Fraud and Save Democracy*, which quickly became one of the most influential books of my life.

I followed up with Veritas every couple of weeks. The election came, and they released their explosive *Rigging the Election* series. I sent over emails asking the Veritas HR recruiter to tell the team congrats. I really wanted the job.

By the time the election happened, I was inspired by both Project Veritas as well as other online commenters who were fighting for free speech in what was becoming a culture war. College campuses had long been progressive training grounds, but when I was in college, people would just protest. Now, those protests were erupting into violence. I picked up *Gorilla Mindset* by Mike Cernovich and started the hard work of overcoming my inner demons. I knew I couldn't remain a victim of my past life events forever, and I desperately wanted to move forward. I applied for other jobs, but Project Veritas was always the one I felt a magnetic pull toward. After the election, I followed up again and heard nothing. I waited two more weeks and sent another email.

By then, it was Thanksgiving, and I spent the holiday at my dad's home in Virginia so I could see my daughter. I told Doug all about Project Veritas and James O'Keefe since I had just finished his book and how I found all of it amazing. Even though we had never met, James seemed like someone who thought the same way I did.

In retrospect, the handful of visits I made to Virginia during that time were all red flags of what was to come. A normal parent would have been thrilled that their daughter, who had been struggling heavily with depression and PTSD, was finally excited about something—anything.

But Doug pooh-poohed my ambitions to work for Project Veritas.

Back in Texas, I happened upon someone on social media who had an extra ticket to the coveted DeploraBall, an inauguration event being hosted by Mike Cernovich and was a veritable who's who of the conservative world. It was the first time I felt like I wanted to be at an event full of people, so I reached out and was gifted the ticket.

I planned my trip so that I would go to Farmville, Virginia, to visit Lexi for a few days before heading to the DC-Baltimore area for the DeploraBall. I even dressed up to attend the event! My anxiety was extremely high, though. Not only was I going to an event full of people, but I was going solo.

Before the event, I spent a couple of days with my best friend from high school, Jessica, who lived in Baltimore. One day, while she was at work, I followed her on the train into DC and went by Arlington National Cemetery where part of Matty's remains were interred.

During the first year following his murder, I heavily felt

his presence. When I visited the cemetery, it was a cold January afternoon at Arlington that day. I sat on the bench in front of where the temporary marker still stood for his memorial. I told him about how I had been trying to move on past his death.

I also told him about Project Veritas. I knew that James O'Keefe would be at the party, and I asked Matty if he thought anything would come of the Project Veritas thing.

I didn't get an answer, but I continued to talk to him like I normally would. I played on a Gameboy and had headphones in to block out any noise. I spent several hours on that bench until the sun started to set and it became too cold for me to be out there.

It felt good to talk to Matty again. I made him a promise that from then on, whenever I was in DC, I'd stop by to see him.

The next day, I went all out to get ready for the event. I got my hair and nails done. I had purchased a formal dress for the first time in nearly a decade. I was still obese from the car accident, but at least I was going to *look* put together.

On the way to the train station, since I was going to Metro in, my parents sent me articles that were already coming up about protests and riots happening outside of the event. I wore a North Face jacket over my formal dress, so it wasn't obvious where I was going. (I did notice some protesters on the same train as me.)

Once off the train, the police already had barricades set up. Party attendees had to show their ticket as well as an ID, and then attendees were directed to proceed on the sidewalk, with protesters directly on the other side of the barrier. When I split off from the protesters, that's when it began.

"SHAME! SHAME! SHAME!"

It really was like an episode of *Game of Thrones*. The police and the Proud Boys in the area helped escort women to the event, so I made it through unscathed, despite having objects hurled at my head along with insults. Never in my life had I seen what should have been a fairly benign political event turn people into such animals. The event wasn't even a fundraiser for Trump and he wouldn't be there.

I suppose that to the crowd, however, the people attending the event were the ones responsible for Donald Trump's victory. It was just so much venom—like nothing I had ever experienced.

I made it to the party but was jarred from what I experienced on the outside. I told myself this was like a final test to see if I had really managed to overcome my agoraphobia. I also told myself I was going to get through the event without the need to take any of the anxiety medication I had been prescribed by doctors.

I did, however, make a beeline for the first bar I saw. I wasn't sure where I was more uncomfortable. On the walk into the event or being at the event, surrounded by happy people smiling, laughing, and talking. I didn't know a soul at the party, and I could feel my social anxiety kicking in as I quickly drank my first Jack and Coke.

Through the noise of the party, I suddenly heard a voice I recognized coming from around a corner. It was James O'Keefe, so I decided that would be a good place to start.

James was seated at a table with several other people, and he was holding court. Just prior to the event, Project Veritas had uncovered a plot to sabotage and put acid in the vents of the party, so he was one of the heroes of the night. At one point, he got up and spoke to a couple of older gentlemen, telling them stories that were in his book, *Breakthrough*. I was so incredibly shy that I looked down at the ground most of the time. It wasn't James's celebrity that did it; it was my own internal struggle of being around that many people. When I found the courage to mention that I had read his book, James smiled, but I looked away and avoided eye contact. People were constantly approaching him wanting to talk, so I knew my chances of having any sort of meaningful conversation with him there were pretty slim.

Talking to a couple of people who were part of his entourage, I mentioned I had applied for the communications role. They looked at each other confused because that role wasn't hiring, but they encouraged me to apply to be a journalist. I didn't talk to them long because I was so self-conscious and worried about appearing weird.

I did meet Mike Cernovich, and he even remembered me from Twitter DMs we had exchanged where I thanked him for his book and how it had helped me to get out of my comfort zone to attend something like the DeploraBall.

I realized later that night that I hadn't asked James to take a photo with me, so I found him and took a selfie with him. It was an incredibly awkward photo and we both look horrible in it, but being able to meet someone I admired so much made the night for me.

I didn't stay long at the party. I overcame mountains by simply attending, but socializing with strangers was just too much for me to bear. I was proud of myself, though. I had met the people whom I wanted to meet and felt that

I made a major breakthrough in recovering from the events of 2015 through 2016.

The next day, I went to the inauguration and watched Donald J. Trump become the forty-fifth president of the United States. It was a new chapter for our country, and I felt like it was also the beginning of a new chapter for me personally.

I didn't end up working for Project Veritas at that time. I applied to be a journalist, but when I realized how much travel the job required, I turned it down in exchange for a much more stable, traditional job.

Still figuring out my place in life, I did a few short stints at different jobs in 2017 before getting an offer for a contract job at Facebook. I was excited and thought this could be the job that changed things for me.

And it was—just not in the way I imagined it would be.

CHAPTER 7

Becoming the Facebook Insider

"CADET SPENCER, STOP GOOFING AROUND ON FACE-book!"

I was often chided by my ROTC instructors for not paying attention in class. I was never the best student in college, so I often jumped on Facebook when I lost interest.

Ironically, my proficiency at using Facebook was one of the things that made me a candidate to become an Army Public Affairs Officer. So when I saw that Facebook had a campus in Texas, I applied, and by the summer of 2017, I accepted a job there. The job was a low-wage content review position. I'm pretty sure the reason I was hired was because I had a college degree and a pulse.

Regardless, I was excited. Sure, it was a contract gig, but it was a start to what I thought my future was going to be. After my military career ended, it seemed like I had the next step in life laid out for me. I was in a tech town working a tech job. In my head, it made sense for me to work at Facebook given that Facebook had, in a way, given me a start in my military career. It felt like things were coming full circle. I thought the contract job would eventually lead to a coveted full-time position where Facebook would see the value in my military officer experience.

Even on day one, I felt like I had somehow "made it." I walked in through the pristine glass doors and was immediately taken with how cheerful and artistic the decor was. Lights hung down from the ceiling and there was art everywhere. It had been Pride Month recently, so there were many rainbow-themed decorations that gave the building a welcoming atmosphere.

An Asian boy sat next to me in the lobby and I could tell he was also waiting to be escorted to his desk. "Nice Super Mario Vans," he said to me. "Are you a sneakerhead?" I laughed and just said I was a nerd.

A bubbly young girl came up to us and gave us the grand tour of the building, showing us where we had access to unlimited snacks, and the amazing cafeteria where the food easily rivaled that of restaurants. For employees and even for contractors, this was all free.

She showed us where we would be sitting—in a large, well-lit open space seated with the rest of our team.

"Oh my God, I love your backpack," said the boy assigned to the desk next to mine about my Hello Kitty backpack. I turned to say thank you and was greeted by a chubby Filipino boy wearing chandelier earrings.

I know it sounds hard to believe, but when I met my coworkers at Facebook, I felt like I had found my people. They were largely a young crowd who seemed quirky and offbeat. Sure, I was aware from day one that politically, we probably identified as opposite parties, but that wasn't new to me. I had been around and been friends with people who didn't agree with me on politics my whole life.

Despite these and any other differences, I actually enjoyed my job at Facebook. I worked the night shift from 4:30 p.m. to 1:00 a.m., so after 6:00 p.m. or 7:00 p.m. when all the other employees went home, the remaining workers had free rein of the office.

Sometimes my coworkers and I would take our laptops and work in a conference room, while watching Dr. Phil. Other nights, we would go into a room with Ping-Pong and video games. On Christmas, we all wore onesies and took pictures next to the Christmas decorations. The boy next to me and I were both obsessed with Korean skincare, so we would do face masks while we worked.

At the time, the night crew had no supervisor on shift, so we really were free to do as we wanted. We still got all of our work done, and when I look back on the time actually working at Facebook, I remember it fondly.

The people at the job, as different as they were from me, made it fun. The job itself was pretty mindless. We were content moderators for intellectual property, so many of the tickets we had were pretty cut and dry.

"Oh, you're live broadcasting a Pay-Per-View event?"

Nope.

"Uploading a Disney movie?"

Also nope.

Some of these tickets were huge. On a given day, I could easily look through over 10,000 pieces of content.

I have mostly fond memories of my coworkers, but that isn't to say my job was without drama or conflict. At some point, a coworker did a deep dive on my personal Facebook account, which was required to be connected to my work account. They saw a picture of a MAGA hat, and I noticed that for a while, everyone was very cold toward me. The guy who was my best friend at the office, Chaz, a gay "bear" whom I bonded with over our mutual love of trash TV and video games, told me about the rumors and gossip that had been going around about me being a Trump supporter. You would have thought that it came out that I was a registered sex offender from the way people acted. I made up an excuse about my ex-husband being extremely conservative and that I had to "live a lie" when I was married to him and was so happy to be free from him.

The whole incident was indicative of the culture war era we live in now. It was bad in 2017, but I know that in 2020, things are far worse, as I watch people who have been friends for decades rip each other apart over political disagreements. Up until the MAGA hat drama, we had all coexisted peacefully, and personally, I had stayed out of any of the high school clique-type drama.

Like I said, the specific area of content review I worked in was intellectual property. So it was a lot of taking down illegal uploads of Disney movies, stopping people from livestreaming Pay-Per-View events, muting videos that had copyrighted music in the background, and so forth.

But sometimes it would include smaller disputes, such as someone posting a photographer's photo without permission. We were tier 1 support, so any tickets that came in that could possibly constitute fair use were escalated to those working in tier 2 or above since, well, we were low-wage contractors.

One night, I got a ticket from a group called the Red Elephants, a conservative page. They were reporting a video from NowThis or Vox, or some other left-wing page, that used their footage to call them alt-right (or something like that).

Even though I was someone who identified as a Republican, I rolled my eyes because as a copyright specialist, I knew this was probably fair use. In order to do my job, I had to look at the pages of both the person making the copyright claim as well as the page that was allegedly violating their copyright.

When I looked at the Red Elephants page, I saw an odd account note that read "IA_LIVEACTION_DEBOOST" in the area that showed all actions taken on the account. It didn't mention that a warning had been sent to the user, which was normal if something like copyright strike was issued to a page.

On each shift, I looked at hundreds of Facebook accounts

and made decisions on thousands of pieces of content, but this was the first time I had ever seen this note on an account.

Most of the content I dealt with was apolitical, so I didn't think much of it at the time.

Then there was a ticket from *The Daily Caller*, the conservative news outlet run by Tucker Carlson at the time. I noticed the same code on their account, too.

A couple of weeks later, I got a ticket from someone who, in addition to managing a professional poker page (which was the content being actioned), was also the ad admin for *Louder with Crowder*'s page, a conservative late-night comedy show hosted by Steven Crowder. I was a regular listener of the show, so out of curiosity, I took a look at the page.

I saw the "IA_LIVEACTION_DEBOOST" appear several times on the account.

Although my work was apolitical, I had gotten copyright claims from left-leaning accounts such as Colin Kaepernick, The Young Turks, Black Lives Matters, and so on. I never saw any actions like that taken on their pages.

I started seeing the beginnings of a pattern. I wanted to

investigate it further, though, before making any definitive conclusions.

Around that same time, James O'Keefe, whom I now kept up with on social media, had tweeted asking anyone who had tips on anything going on at the Big Tech companies, including the one where I worked, to email Project Veritas.

I was at home lying in bed when I saw the tweet and shot over an email. I said I wasn't sure if I had anything of particular value but that I'd be willing to speak to them about my experiences.

I was surprised at how quickly someone got back to me. They arranged a call and asked me questions about my job. I mentioned what I had been noticing but said I wasn't 100 percent sure that it was politically motivated yet. I definitely downplayed it all on the phone call because there was a part of me that wondered if I really wanted to go down this rabbit hole. I was doing really well at my job at Facebook. The team I was on was rapidly growing and my numbers were good, so if I stuck with it, there were opportunities for advancement and even a coveted role as a Facebook full-time employee.

I had been through so much, between my brother's death, my latest divorce, and Matty's murder. I was still recovering from fairly severe PTSD. I was finally getting settled in Texas and looked forward to having my daughter join me once she finished elementary school.

But the part of me that told me I had to do the right thing kept nagging at me. I didn't have anything for sure yet, but I knew the issue was an important one, since companies like Facebook, Google, and Twitter essentially have a monopoly in our online discourse, and if certain viewpoints were being suppressed, it wasn't right.

Sometime around Halloween of 2017, I remember sitting at my favorite ramen spot in Austin, waiting to meet with a gentleman from Project Veritas. It was a spot in a hip neighborhood, so a straitlaced, middle-aged man stood out.

Ken, as he told me his name was, introduced himself and asked more about me, my life, and why I decided to reach out. We talked a little about the stuff I had noticed at Facebook, and he gave me some suggestions on encrypted apps to use to communicate with him from then on.

His background was in law enforcement, so I felt a certain kinship with him as someone who had previously served as a military officer. I've noticed those who have worked in the uniformed services tend to gel well. He seemed to like how methodical I was in noting what I had observed at Facebook, and he asked me about my family, growing up in Hawaii, and what working at Facebook was like as far as the culture and the people.

After lunch, we walked to a park area nearby, and he pulled out a small hard-shelled case from his bag. Inside was a hidden camera. He encouraged me to document the things I had been observing. I looked at the device and knew that I was about to make a decision that was going to change the rest of my life.

"You do realize that once I do this, I'll never be able to get a security clearance job again."

* * *

But the voice in my head continued to nag at me. The more instances of the deboost code I observed, the more obvious it was about what was going on at Facebook. I couldn't just ignore it.

Facebook has over two billion users around the world. This code was being run on the back end of the platform, and users were having their content suppressed without their knowledge. Users are not Facebook's consumers—they (and their personal data) are the *product*. Facebook, by design, made themselves the new public square, and the public allowed Facebook to farm all their data, thinking that in exchange, they were being given an open platform to talk and conduct business. They weren't.

And the public had a right to know.

CHAPTER 8

The Investigation

I HAD NEVER WORKED AS AN UNDERCOVER ANY-
thing, so using the hidden camera was very foreign to me.
I tried to be creative in making it work with the clothing I
would normally wear, but it seemed most of my footage
would usually be of the ceiling or of the ground. I didn't
have any way of reviewing the footage since my computer
wasn't set up for that and most days there wasn't much
of anything to see.

I intentionally looked for tickets that involved political
and media figures, on both the left and the right, that
had those strange account notes. One time, I got a look
at Mike Cernovich's page, the same person whose book
Gorilla Mindset had helped me heal from my PTSD, and
the deboost code appeared at least a dozen times.

I mentioned earlier that Facebook forces employees to connect their internal workplace accounts to their personal Facebook pages. This allows employees to look at internal groups and keep up with things from home. I couldn't access the back ends of people's pages from my house, but I began to look into various policy groups and documents within Facebook and scoured them for evidence of political bias.

Like many internet rabbit holes, I would find one thing and then stay up until six in the morning researching and researching, going deeper and deeper in the hole. I then faithfully submitted everything that I documented to Ken. Sometimes he would say the team had follow-up questions to help understand the things I was sending over, such as what certain acronyms meant, for example.

I never questioned whether Ken was actually passing the information along or not. After all, I had no reason to not trust him.

* * *

In December, I got a package in the mail with a signed copy of James's book, *Breakthrough*, and a note from James saying he appreciated what I was doing. Enclosed, there was a copy of his business card, and he had written his cell phone number on the back.

Right after Christmas, I went home to Maui to spend a week on vacation at my grandfather's house with my daughter. By this time, I had sent well over fifty pages of documentation to Project Veritas, and the evidence I had gathered was pretty solid.

I was going through my phone sending people Happy New Year texts with a picture of the bicoastal views from my grandmother's house and the Maui sunset in the background when I came upon James's number, which I had saved in my phone as "Aaron from Tinder."

I thought about it and figured why not wish him a Happy New Year? So I sent him the same text I had sent several other people. He sent me a picture wearing a tuxedo from a party he was attending in New York City. I laughed and sent him a picture I had taken from my aunt's farm earlier that day of me holding a baby goat and said that his New Year's looked more glamorous than mine.

That was it. That was the entire conversation. Not a word about Facebook or any of the work I was doing. I didn't think it was a big deal. The conversation was completely innocent. A couple of days later, however, I got a somewhat accusatory email from Ken asking how I got James's number.

"Um, he gave it to me."

He told me that I was now forbidden from talking to him and that from now on, any communication was strictly to go through him.

Considering what happened next, this seemed reasonable.

CHAPTER 9

Getting Fired from Facebook

IT WAS AN ABNORMALLY WARM DAY IN AUSTIN FOR January. The temperatures had risen back up to 80°F, so I decided not to wear the hoodie I had rigged with a hidden camera.

It had been an exciting couple of days for me to continue investigating Facebook because two days prior, Project Veritas had released their exposé into Twitter. They had Twitter employees admit on hidden camera footage to "shadow banning" people, among other things.

On Workplace, Facebook's back end, there were several global discussion groups and a few threads talking about the piece and warning employees to be careful about discussing company policy in bars, and so forth.

I set my bag down, and my manager told me that they needed to talk to me in the conference room. I didn't think anything of it, so I dropped down my Hello Kitty backpack, grabbed a bottle of water, and met them inside.

Across from the table were both of my managers as well as two representatives from BCForward, the subcontracting company I technically worked for. I knew this wasn't going to be a good meeting, as the door locked behind me.

"You're being terminated."

I slowly blinked. I always knew this was a possibility, but I was kind of in shock that it was happening.

"Can I ask why?"

* * *

"The client won't say. Something about a security issue."

"Well, that seems kind of unfair that I'm not even being told *why* I'm being terminated. If I'm being accused of something, I feel like I should at least know what I've allegedly done that's wrong."

"Facebook security also wants to see your cell phone."

"Wait...What? My *personal* cell phone?"

This was particularly egregious to me since although I completely understood the desire to have back their company property, asking for my personal cell phone, on which I did no Facebook business, was a definite overreach.

"If I do, can I keep my job?"

There was absolutely nothing of importance regarding Facebook or Project Veritas on my cell phone. Despite knowing that I needed to expose the censorship at Facebook, I also really needed to be able to pay my rent. If they looked through the phone, the only thing they would have found were the silly Happy New Year's texts to James. He wasn't in my phone as James O'Keefe, but telling James O'Keefe Happy New Year's certainly did not seem like a fireable offense.

"No."

I scrunched up my face as I looked at them. They wanted to completely invade my privacy far beyond what would be reasonable for an employer for nothing in exchange.

"Facebook security said you can look over their shoulder while they go through your phone."

"This is *my* cell phone. It isn't company property."

I reiterated that I would like to know what I had been accused of and asked if there was going to be an internal investigation that (at least I acted like) would have cleared me.

The "We want to see your phone," "If I let you see my phone" circle lasted for what felt like hours.

"If I can't keep my job, and I don't mean this to be disrespectful, then why the hell would I let you look through my personal phone?"

The conversation continued to go nowhere and finally, exasperated, I said, "Clearly, this conversation isn't going anywhere. Can I go now?"

"Well, legally we can't detain you."

I looked at the BCForward guy like an arm had grown out of his forehead. *Detain* me? In all my years of being in the military, I never imagined that at a civilian company, I would be facing this kind of treatment.

Facebook security escorted me out of the building, not

even allowing me to go back to my desk to clear my belongings. I walked to the parking garage across the street stunned, angry, and confused. The first call I made was to Ken, my handler at Project Veritas, who said he would call me with instructions on what to do next shortly. Then I called my dad. I'll never forget the first question he asked me.

"Was it worth it?"

Without a beat of hesitation, I answered yes. I knew that I had done the right thing. I had solid proof that Facebook was engaging in political censorship. I didn't know what any of it really meant in the bigger picture. At the time, I had never heard of the Communications Decency Act or the potential legal ramifications if Facebook were forced to admit that they were a publisher, like *The New York Times*, versus a neutral platform, like, let's say, the phone company. All I knew is that I had seen something that had seemed off to me, investigated it further, and after looking at the back ends of hundreds of accounts, found that it was in fact a pattern of political censorship.

With a user base of over two billion people, the public had a right to know.

That night, my roommate, Casey, brought me ice cream. He tried to comfort me as I cried about being fired. Ken told me that I needed to destroy my cell phone, which pained me because it was the brand-new iPhone X that had just come out.

We took the phone out into the back and smashed it with a hammer. The phone then caught on fire, something Ken warned us could happen, and the hose didn't put it out, so we picked up the flaming remnants of my iPhone with tongs and dropped it into a pot of water. After letting it sit overnight, we threw the rest out with the dirty cat litter.

Ken told me to purchase a burner phone at Walmart using cash, so I did. I was told to change all my passwords and to avoid any use of social media, particularly Facebook, so I did. Because my phone was so new, I wasn't able to get a replacement for over a week. I was cut off from my family, I didn't know who of my friends to trust, and I relied so heavily on social media to receive information as well as send it that I felt like I had been cut off from the outside world.

Although we have no proof, for the next several days, my roommate and I saw a suspicious car not normally parked on our street. I knew I had just done something that would likely anger one of the richest and most powerful corporations in the world, so I had most of my meals delivered to the house and avoided leaving.

A week before I had been fired, I had taken a trial dance lesson at a ballroom dance studio in Austin. Getting over a fear of dancing in public was a New Year's resolution I had made that year. Realizing it was too late to cancel my appointment, a few days after I had been fired, I reluctantly went to my lesson.

CHAPTER 10

David

BEFORE I WENT INTO MY FIRST "FREE TRIAL" lesson at the dance studio, I wrote down the name of the instructor I would be meeting with. I read his bio on the website:

> David is inarguably a Texan, through and through! Born and raised in Houston, David led the exciting life of an amateur bull-rider-turned-deputy-sheriff, and is now a full-time dance instructor. While on the rodeo circuit, David's visits to local nightclubs sparked a desire to join the dance crowd. He began taking dance lessons in 1994 and soon began teaching part time and competing in the Country Western circuit. He has nearly two decades of teaching experience and numerous national and world titles under his belt. David presently competes in the Country Western and West Coast Swing national circuits professionally and

with students. He enjoys working with students toward their Showcase performance goals as well as teaching students who want to improve their social dancing.

"Dancing is hard. If dancing were easy, it would be called football!"

His sense of humor (and rodeo-clowning experience!) shine through in David's high-energy teaching style. As an instructor, David approaches lessons with a keen sense of technique and enforces the importance of posture and the dancer's core as the center of movement. A student's smile is as important to him as their posture! He truly finds his joy in dancing, and is always grateful to see the happiness dance brings out in his students.

When I first met David, I was extremely nervous since dancing was something I was never good at. My father always said I was "accident prone," and I was born severely pigeon-toed to the point where as a child, I had to wear foot braces at night. Because of this, dance was not something that came naturally to me—at all. In fact, dancing may have been the one thing that was more foreign to me than the world of the military.

Although so much of my life seems like one unplanned chaotic mess after the next, David being assigned as my instructor was one of those acts of destiny I feel like that came in my life intentionally. When we first met, he recognized the nerdy reference on my T-shirt, and I noted that his wedding band had a Batman logo on it. David was about the same age as my older brother, and something about him put me at ease very quickly. He encouraged me to try group classes as well as take private dance lessons, but I couldn't at the time of the first lesson since at Facebook, I worked 4:30 p.m. to 1:00 a.m., including most weekends.

When I showed up to that second lesson, it was the first time I had talked to someone other than my roommate in days. I have no idea what came over me at the time, but in that instant, I decided to trust David. I told him I had been fired from Facebook, and then I told him everything. Of course, this man had just met me about a week prior, so he probably thought I was crazy. Regardless, he once again encouraged me to take group classes since I suddenly now found my evenings and weekends freed up. So I did.

Over the course of the next few months, I took, on average, twenty group classes a week on top of a weekly private lesson with David. At the time, I had heard little to nothing from Ken, and I didn't know what to do with myself. Getting up to attend dance classes gave me *something* to do during the day, a reason to get up out of bed and to leave my house.

With David's encouragement, I kept myself busy enough to take my mind off the pain, and through taking the group classes I began to at least talk to people again. I've always been extremely introverted and socially anxious (and to be honest, I still am) and the whole Facebook firing scenario, along with the silence from Project Veritas, exacerbated my discomfort with other people and my PTSD.

I was moving through life in such a haze at the time and dancing allowed me to come out of my shell. Aside from David, I kept the truth about what had happened at Facebook a secret.

After dancing for a couple of months, during my private lesson with David, he asked, "Do you want to do West Coast Swing with me?" I said sure, thinking he just wanted to work on that for that day's lesson. Before I knew it, however, I was signing papers and paying a deposit to perform in a showcase. I felt bamboozled.

When the time came to perform, it was the first time I had done anything in the performing arts in over a decade. I panicked and drank heavily beforehand. After looking at the video later, despite my dancing being incredibly awkward, I had a great time.

I knew that David competed in Pro-Am dance competitions with some of his students. This allowed amateur students, such as myself, to compete with professional dancers where only they would be graded so they can get into competitions without having to find a dance partner who was around the same skill level, or at least willing to work with someone who had less than a year of experience. Along with my justice complex, I slowly felt my love for the performing arts coming back. If James and his book *Breakthrough* were to thank for reigniting the spark in me to pursue justice, then David was to thank for reigniting the spark that made me love to perform.

At this point in time, I still hadn't heard anything from Project Veritas. I needed an outlet to pour my energy into, and I decided dance was it.

CHAPTER 11

Silence Is Deafening

KEN HAD TOLD ME TO STAND BY FOR FURTHER instructions following my termination from Facebook. The company hadn't even let me clear out my desk, so I had been emailing back and forth with my managers and the BCForward people to figure out how to get my belongings back. There was nothing of any interest to Facebook in my desk. I just wanted back my headphones, pictures of my daughter, and assorted knickknacks I had decorated with.

Almost two weeks after my termination, I still hadn't heard from Veritas, nor did I have my stuff back from Facebook. Frustrated, I sent Jeffrey from BCForward an email stating that if my things weren't returned within forty-eight hours, I would call the Austin police to have them escort me to get my personal belongings back. Finally, they said they had boxed up my stuff, and Jeffrey offered to meet me at a Starbucks. I didn't know Jeffrey very well, but he was one of the corporate representatives who sat down in the room with me while I was being interrogated and had given me his card before I went home.

This time, I did not make the mistake of not wearing a hidden camera. I wanted Project Veritas to know the firing had gone exactly like I had described. My instincts for journalism kicked in, and I intentionally went inside to wait in line so Jeffrey couldn't just meet me in the parking lot to give me my things. In the Starbucks line, we had the following conversation:

> Me: How's everything going? Sorry if the email was a little heavy-handed; it's just because it's been a week and a half.

> Jeffrey: I don't know what's going on. They're still working on the investigation, getting all the details from what I've gotten.

> Me: Yeah, is this like normal? Because I asked some of my buddies who still work there, and they said management hasn't said *anything* about me even being off the team. I have no clue what's going on or why I was let go.

> Jeffrey: Yeah, we're still getting more information now, but

we're still kind of waiting, 'cause they didn't give us anything when we came in.

Me: Yeah, you guys seemed to be as clueless as I was. I would get mad at somebody if I knew who to get mad at.

Jeffrey: Yeah, we're just the bad guys delivering the news. My boss who lives in Indy [BCForward is based in Indianapolis, Indiana] wants to talk about it this afternoon, about what we need to do, so I'm sure there'll be an update. I mean, we can't just let you go and not give you a reason. There's a reason behind everything, and I don't know why they were being so sketchy about it. We're trying to figure that out now.

Me: Well, I appreciate it.

Jeffrey: They're just keeping us in the dark.

Me: Yeah, I mean, even the cell phone thing seemed odd. Is that normal?

Jeffrey: It's the first time I've ever seen it. They were like, "We need to ask if we can see the phone," but they needed your permission since they're not legally allowed to do that.

Me: I don't really have anything to hide, but it'd be one thing to let them see my phone if I was going to keep my job.

Jeffrey: Yeah, that was weird. We were just following their orders. It would have been easier for us if they had given us reasons for your termination, but no. We're in the dark.

Me: So do you think Accenture [BCForward was a subcontractor of Accenture] knows what happened?

Jeffrey: No, like I told you, we get the call, and they haven't told us anything. They said they can't share anything with you. They're leaving us in the dark with whatever happened. And what sucks is that it could have just been nothing.

Me: Yeah, I mean, I half expect them to be like, "Oh, oops!"

Jeffrey: Exactly! Like what could it possibly be that's causing all this?

In the two weeks since my firing, I had won an unemployment claim against BCForward since I was never given a reason for my termination. BCForward therefore had a vested interest in getting me back to work again as soon as possible. They had another contract doing content review for YouTube (a Google-owned company). After I got my things from him, Jeffrey said that they wanted to move me to that project and asked me to check back in with him about when I could start.

CHAPTER 12

Hard Times

WHEN I WAS FIRED IN JANUARY OF 2018, I WAS already barely making it on my meager salary, but at least I was getting free meals, so my food costs were very low.

Losing a job where I was paid weekly, and was barely making it, put me in a bad position. My roommate had also recently lost his job, and financially, we were screwed. We had enough money to last another month or two (maybe) before we would no longer be able to pay our rent.

At that point, my instincts to survive kicked in, and I would do whatever it took to get by. Pride went out the window. So I did something that I had never done before— not during my time in college, not as a single mother, not ever.

I applied for food stamps while I was on unemployment. This was the first time I had applied for, or required, any kind of assistance from the government. It went against all my principles, and it was mortifying. I reminded myself that this was temporary and that it wasn't going to be a permanent solution or a lifestyle choice for me.

Like when I was agoraphobic, I would only go to the store in the middle of the night and would use the self-checkout in hopes that no one would see me using an EBT card.

Jeffrey told me BCForward would have a position for me on another contract, but I had to wait. I waited six weeks, but it felt like six months.

Throwing myself into dance was my only saving grace during this time. Luckily, they had new student specials that allowed me to take as many classes as I wanted for a low cost. If not for that, I'm not sure how I would have kept myself from falling back into the mental health gutter I knew I was teetering dangerously close to.

Later, when *Business Insider* would claim I had been "planted" by Project Veritas at Facebook, a claim they would later have to retract and now sits on the Wall of Shame at the Project Veritas office, I think back to that time of economic uncertainty and laugh. If I had been a plant or had intentionally gone to Facebook to leak documents, I wouldn't have ended up in such dire straits.

After that seemingly endless six weeks, I began another tech contract gig, this time at Google. I was initially supposed to review content for YouTube, but on my first day of work, several other members of my "class" and I discovered that they had overhired for that team, so we would instead be doing customer support for YouTube TV, Google's cable TV replacement service.

Already, after having experienced what life was actually like at a tech company, I felt a little jaded. But walking inside this facility was a different feeling entirely. We were tucked away in a building in an industrial park, far from downtown Austin. There were no signs that indicated that we were at a Google facility. The decor was tacky, and a heavy feeling hung in the air that I can only describe as depression.

It was at this job that I was introduced to one of tech's dirty secrets—the thousands of low-skill, low-wage subcontract workers at major tech companies.

Magazines such as *Forbes* and movies such as *The Internship* glamorize these tech campuses and all the amazing perks available. And to be perfectly honest, the Facebook facility where I had worked, which was staffed mainly by Facebook full-time employees, fit the bill.

But this wasn't a fun, hip place to work. It was what I called a contractor farm. There was a medium-sized cafeteria on the ground floor, but the food wasn't free. There was a gym, but it required an additional membership you had to pay for. There were snacks but with a selection maybe one-fifth the size of the micro-kitchens at Facebook. There were no kegs of cold brew coffee or alcohol on-site either.

Instead of an open floor plan that encouraged you to get to know and socialize with your coworkers, the floor was a sea of cubicles. Since we worked in what was essentially a call center, it operated 24/7, and the agents didn't have their own cubicles they could decorate to make them a little less depressing. Being there felt like being stuck in a Dilbert cartoon or a scene from Office Space.

Despite the things that happened at Facebook, the constant propaganda, the company culture that eschewed any kind of deviation from corporate dogma, it was at least a pleasant place to work. This place, on the other hand, was the complete opposite. I hated that job from the very first day.

A few months after I began at the Google contractor farm, the dance studio where I had been training advertised they were looking to hire new instructors. They placed an emphasis that dance experience and ability were not the main factors they were looking for, so I applied.

By then, it was the summer of 2018, and I was looking forward to having my daughter back home with me. I thought that a career as a dance teacher would allow me to have a job where if I had to bring her with me after school, I could since a ballroom dance studio is a perfectly wholesome place for a kid to hang out. There were teenagers who trained at the studio as well, so I thought that if they had the discipline to ballroom dance, they were probably responsible enough to be decent babysitters as well.

To my surprise, I was accepted into the instructor training program, and I began to train to be a dance teacher. During my time on unemployment and food stamps, dance was the one light spot in a dark time in my life. I looked forward to bringing some of the joy that dance had brought to me to other people, even though I knew I would have to step my game up since my actual dance skills were, well, practically nonexistent.

And I still hadn't heard anything from anyone at Project Veritas. It had been months. Not only was I confused, but I also felt hurt and used. I did the best to pick up the pieces of my life and forge ahead.

If nothing else, I had learned to be adaptable.

CHAPTER 13

A Pivotal Choice

MAY 24, 2018, AUSTIN, TEXAS

"FYI, I AM LEAVING PV [PROJECT VERITAS] THIS week," Ken wrote to me in an email. I was shocked. "I have been asked to forward your emails to Joe. Which I will do in an email introduction tomorrow. I think we should have a phone conversation before you actually respond to him."

Ken also mentioned a potential writing job he was willing to refer me for and asked me not to tell Project Veritas anything about it or mention the email to them.

The email was confusing. I quickly realized the Joe he was referring to was Joe Halderman, the executive producer for Project Veritas. I looked him up on Wikipedia and found out he had done time in Rikers for allegedly blackmailing David Letterman.

Since I had discovered the corporate malfeasance at Facebook and got involved with Project Veritas, nothing good had happened to me. Having to apply for food stamps was probably the most humiliating thing I had ever done in my life. I was working a job I hated, in a call center, but was on track to work a job as a dance teacher that although not financially lucrative in the slightest, would have made me happier. Did I really want anything to do with any of these people?

Ken sent the email introduction and I didn't respond, as he instructed.

JUNE 6, 2018, PFLUGERVILLE, TEXAS

I was walking around in a Walmart when Ken finally called me. He proceeded to tell me how James and everyone at Project Veritas were horrible reckless people and that because of their incompetence, myself and several other sources had been burned in groups like Antifa.

Ken told me the reason I was fired from Facebook was because James told his ex-girlfriend about me, whose cousin worked at Facebook, and the reason I ended up in the dire position I did rested squarely on James's shoulders.

He told me James O'Keefe was a "textbook narcissist" and that he was the reason Ken and his colleague Richard had left the company. He told me the two of them were working to secure funding for their own venture, and he would like to bring me on board due to my military intelligence and tech backgrounds.

In his words, not mine, he told me that they would be a "pay for play" operation that would be hired by clients. We would then go undercover looking for information, but because we were essentially hired guns, any information gathered would be delivered to the client, and it was up to them what to do with it. He said we would go out on a job, work for a few months, then be off for a few months, and that it would be financially lucrative.

At the time, I had no reason to believe that anything Ken had told me was a lie. He had been the one to fly down to Austin once a month to check in and see how things were going as I investigated the corruption at Facebook. He was an older man and had a "dad" air about him. It made you want to trust him.

After the conversation, I responded to the email introducing me to Joe. I didn't hear anything back right away, and at the time, I took it as a sign that Ken was in fact telling me the truth—that Project Veritas had chewed me up and spit me out, leaving me to fend for myself in Texas.

Joe called me a couple of weeks later. He had horrific timing since I was about to take a master Two Step workshop because I thought I was done with Project Veritas. An anxiety and tightness built up in my chest while I tried to sound casual and unbothered on the phone. But in my head, I thought about the Wikipedia article. This man was a criminal and a stranger. *This* was the person I was supposed to trust?

I explained the things that had happened at Facebook as well as I could over the phone, but he seemed confused, like he hadn't seen the documents. He did seem far nicer than I expected him to be, and at the end of the conversation, we agreed I should fly to New York to go over what I had found, and we'd take it from there.

If I were to write things down on paper, I should have just trusted Ken and ignored Project Veritas. But something in my heart told me to at least go to New York and see what they had to say.

As one might expect, I can't remember a single thing I learned in that Two Step workshop that day.

CHAPTER 14

Mamaroneck, New York

JULY 4, 2018, NEW YORK CITY

I GOT TO WATCH THE FOURTH OF JULY FIREWORKS as my flight landed at JFK Airport. I hadn't been back to New York in years, and it was a beautiful reminder of all the things that our country stands for. Admittedly, I was excited. Ever since reading *Breakthrough*, there was something unexplainable that I felt had drawn me to James O'Keefe. It just felt like he was someone who shared my worldview and ideals.

I had one picture of James O'Keefe in my mind based on the book, the very brief interaction we had at a party over a year prior, on what Ken had said, and the articles I read about James in the media. I didn't know what I was about to get into.

Who was the real James O'Keefe?

The next morning, I headed to Project Veritas's office. When I arrived, I looked around to take it all in. Understandably, people who worked at Project Veritas are wary of strangers, so several people gawked when I came in. Since Joe was out of town, a well-dressed young man named Brian greeted me and had me take a seat in a conference room. He left to go take care of something, and I was alone for what felt like an eternity. I spun around in the office chair and wondered to myself how many cameras were probably pointed at me. I didn't want to play with my phone and have them think I was suspicious. On the walls, there were articles and memorabilia commemorating some of Project Veritas's victories over the years. I looked around and stared up at the ceiling, thinking back on all the events that had led me here.

Brian came back into the room. He had copies of the documents I had sent from Facebook, and I began to explain the dashboard on the back end, where the account notes were and where I saw "IA_LIVEACTION_DEBOOST" and the name "Danny Ben David." I knew that these were actions taken by Facebook on a user's account because it was the same area where content reviewers also took action against an account when giving them a copyright strike, removing content for violating community guidelines, and so on.

I explained the internal "troll report" I found that specifically talked about targeting conservatives without naming them as such. I also explained the research I had done on the authors of the report, even though they worked at the Menlo Park campus in California and I was at a Facebook facility in downtown Austin, Texas.

We left the conference room, and I was sitting at a desk when James came walking in the door. He looked at me and said, "You must be the girl from Facebook." I nodded. "I look forward to talking to you," he said. Then he looked down at the Apple Watch I was wearing and said, "I don't trust those things."

I looked at him like he was nuts. Was he really questioning me after all the things I had gone through? Maybe Ken was right. I somewhat sarcastically took the watch off and made a big show of dropping it into my backpack.

"There. Happy?"

James set his things down in his office, and shortly thereafter, the three of us were walking to lunch. We went to a small pizza place in Mamaroneck, New York. James asked if I had any food preferences, and I said no.

So much had gone into making this meeting happen, and I had many things on my mind. I was going to give Veritas the Facebook documents, but was I going to discuss how they had basically abandoned me? I was trying to analyze the whole situation in my mind, examining every word out of James's mouth, every small behavior, trying to determine if the things Ken said were true.

James asked me about everything that had transpired at Facebook, and when it came to my firing, I summoned up all the courage I had and said, "Well, you would know. I heard from someone that it's because you told your ex-girlfriend who has a cousin who works at Facebook."

James looked at me, completely deadpan, with an expression that I would soon refer to as James O'Keefe's patented WTF face.

"What in the world are you talking about?"

Call it a gut instinct, but it was clear this man had no clue what I was talking about. I made the life-changing decision in that moment that I was going to trust James O'Keefe. On the one hand, James was a man I didn't know, a man whom I had heard horrible things about, and a man who had allegedly been one of the reasons that the first part of 2018 had been so hard for me. On the other hand, through reading his book, I felt like I understood him to an extent, and were it not for the inspiration I drew from his work, I would not have had the courage to blow the whistle on one of the most powerful corporations on planet Earth.

I have always been a somewhat impulsive and reactionary type of person, from my decisions to get married, to deciding to suddenly shift gears and try my hand at becoming a dancer, and this was one of those moments where I decided the best thing to do was to lay out all my cards on the table.

I told James *everything*.

To James's knowledge, Ken had left the company as a "friend," and so had his friend Richard, whom I had never met or talked to. I told James about the horrible things Ken had said about him, about the weird scheme they were planning, and how Ken told me that James personally was the reason I ended up jobless and on food stamps. James was in such shock that he called his assistant and told her to push back all his calls and meetings because this was now taking priority.

The things I told James regarding people he had trusted

were so outrageous that at times he didn't believe me. So I pulled out my phone and showed him the texts, emails, and so on. He turned to Brian, who had been quiet most of lunch, and said that this afternoon, our job was to print copies of everything—all of the Facebook documents as well as all the correspondence I had between Ken and me.

James was quieter on the walk back to the office after lunch. When we were inside, I sat down and looked up at him and he said, "Please, Cassandra, please believe me when I say that if I had any idea of what was going on, I would have flown down there personally to take care of it myself. I am so sorry for what you've had to go through. I didn't know what was happening, but since it's my company, I feel responsible. I don't know how you could ever forgive me, but I really appreciate you and what you've done."

I spent the afternoon forwarding all the emails to Brian from my phone since I didn't have a laptop at the time. At one point, I accidentally forwarded an email Ken had sent me back to Ken.

"Got an email from you today that was the same email you sent a while back. Not sure if you're trying to send something. You doing okay? Have a good 4th?"

"Yup! Just busy with dance. They're putting me in an

instructor training program. How's everything on your end?"

"Not bad. Hoping to build an ammunition plant in Colo."

"That's awesome!"

That was the last I ever heard from Ken.

James would occasionally stop by between meetings and calls to check on Brian and my progress. Sometimes he would stop and we'd talk for a while. James wanted to know why in the world, after everything I had been through, I still wanted to help them.

The whole trip had been extremely overwhelming, and so I fumbled over my words. At times, it felt like I was being interrogated. I knew why I had helped him, but during that initial trip to New York, I just had trouble putting it into words. I've always been socially awkward, and talking to James, who at 6'2" towered over me, was even more awkward since my mind had trouble processing the things I had heard about James from Ken, or what I had read in articles, from the man I began to get to know that day.

The next morning, we all met early at the office for breakfast, and I went over the documents again in excruciating detail. The staff had clearly never seen them (thanks again, Ken) and the Communications Director, Stephen Gordon, said, "We already have the story. The documents *are* the story."

Since up until then, Project Veritas had only done undercover exposés, this was new to everyone. This was the first time that someone from inside an organization had leaked information to Project Veritas. Everyone was a little confused as to why I was sitting there in the office. I was so bewildered by the events of the past few months that I myself was still wondering what I was doing. All the actions I had taken at that point were on pure instinct. If I had to put words into the mouth of my internal monologue, it was this: *This is the right thing to do.*

I was in New York for only part of a day after that initial meeting because I needed to get back to Texas. My daughter was finally coming home, and I felt a certain sense of closure that I had figured out what had happened with Project Veritas. I had a new career path that I was really looking forward to as a dance instructor, and until I had enough work doing that, I could keep working at Google, and my family, meaning my daughter and me, would be put back together.

Before I left, James said, "Right now, our relationship is based on mutually assured destruction. I hope that changes someday."

We just stared at each other for a minute, I think each gauging the other person's sincerity in all the words that had been spoken over the course of my trip to New York.

CHAPTER 15

The Ultimate Betrayal

I FLEW BACK TO AUSTIN AFTER THAT WHIRLWIND trip a little bewildered by everything I had just experienced. I thought of myself as someone rather ordinary in many respects, but the past two days had been wild.

I didn't have much time to dwell on it, though, because it was now time to go from Project Veritas mode back into mom mode. My daughter had been living away from me while I got settled in Texas, and I was so excited for her to be coming home. I had her enrolled in the local middle school and met with her guidance counselor and teachers to discuss some of my concerns since my daughter was coming from a small private school and jumping into a large public school in Texas. I had asked her what kind of day camp she'd like to do during the rest of the summer since school wasn't starting for another month. She said she wanted to do acting, so I enrolled her in a theater camp that was being held at the dance studio during the day. It was perfect.

The night before Lexi's return, I went with my dance friends to Wild West, a country bar with a large dance floor. Dancing had become a refuge and an escape from all the craziness that had happened that year. I texted Jason, and he said that he and Lexi would make the drive to Texas from Alabama (where Lexi had been having her annual summer visitation with her dad) early the next morning, and he'd let me know once he was on the road.

I woke up in the morning, and there was no text from Jason.

I called, and there was no answer.

I tried not to panic right away. Maybe Jason forgot to text before they left, and they were driving through an area with no service. They were scheduled to arrive in the late afternoon or early evening.

As each hour ticked by, I began to get more and more nervous. I called and texted, but in return, there was radio silence.

At this point in time, I thought Jason and I had a good relationship. A couple of years prior, when he was still in the Army and I was still in California, he had spent a weekend at my place, and we had Thanksgiving dinner at my mom's house near Sacramento. When I had to go with my reserve unit to Fort Irwin out in the desert for training, Jason would stop by and bring me Powerade and snacks, and we would hang out.

We married very young and also divorced very young. I didn't (and to this day still do not) hold a lot of personal animosity toward Jason.

Jason had gotten out of the Army some time before that summer and had been trying to find his footing as a civilian ever since. I completely understood the struggle, so when he fell behind on child support, I didn't think of it as a big deal. Jason and I were both going through transformative phases in our lives, and Lexi was living with my wealthy father, so it's not like I had an urgent need for the money anyway.

However, after the Facebook incident, I was broke, so when I needed to spend over $2,000 on day camps for Lexi, I asked Jason to help me. I told him to send me anything, even if it was nominal, so at least I felt like he was trying to help.

Sometime around Lexi's birthday in June, he told me he thought that Lexi should stay in Virginia.

Earlier in May, my father, Doug, had suggested the same thing. However, it had been two years—I was clearly happy living in Austin despite the upheavals. And Lexi was about to begin middle school, so the "let her finish elementary school here" argument no longer held weight.

It was 2018, the same year I realized how much I let Doug influence and control many aspects of my life. For as long as I could remember, I had gone back and forth between doing things to follow in his footsteps to make him proud, such as speech and debate, and rebelling to try and forge my own path, such as joining the Army instead of becoming an attorney like him.

Some additional background on Doug: As I mentioned in the first chapter, when I was a child, my parents were picture-perfect, late-'80s and early '90s yuppies. Doug was Honolulu's second largest personal injury attorney and drove a Porsche, and I spent my early years growing up in a mansion, complete with pool, private tennis court, and live-in help—the whole deal.

Doug was also a womanizer. My mother, Karen, I found out as a teenager, was his third wife. I knew he had been married once prior to my mom but only found out about wife number two my senior year of high school from an older cousin of mine. To this day, he has cheated on every woman I have ever known him to be with. When my mom was pregnant with my younger brother, he had an affair with his secretary. Classy guy.

My parents threw lavish parties at the mansion, and I remember (more than once) waking up to come downstairs and see beer cans floating in the pool. My parents were Honolulu socialites, and they always made sure that I attended the "right" schools and did the "right" things.

When I think back on it now, in many ways Doug was a very Patrick Bateman à la *American Psycho* type of character. At 5'3", Doug was, and still is, the poster child for Napoleon syndrome. He was extremely successful, ruthlessly so, driven out of a desire to prove all those who doubted him wrong.

Although my parents always provided me with the best and brightest opportunities, there was a cold, Stepford quality to my family life.

Around age ten, my family decided to move to Maui, where much of my extended family lived. It was around this time that we began going to church, and Doug, quite suddenly, turned into a very different person. He became deeply religious and conservative—and I don't just mean that in the political sense.

I recall, for a time in middle school, not being allowed to watch Disney movies because they supported gay rights.

I also remember having to listen to a sermon from a "converted" homosexual and a speaker encouraging not only waiting until marriage to have sex but to wait until marriage to kiss, and this wasn't even the most extreme.

The worst speaker talked about all sorts of crazy conspiracies, half of which didn't make sense to me at age fourteen. I distinctly remember the speaker advised his audience to not get driver's licenses or pay taxes because we were living in the end times.

Now that we are all adults, my friends told me they were always scared of Doug. The slightest thing could cause him to blow up and start yelling at everyone.

Doug had three children. Jeremy, from his first marriage, was always the black sheep. His mom was Doug's high school sweetheart, and Nancy was married to Doug when he was poor and still in college and then law school. As a result, Jeremy reaped very little of the benefits of Doug's later success. I was taught to view Jeremy as a disappointment, a welfare queen, and a loser.

My youngest brother, Thornton, as I mentioned before, fell into drugs at a very young age. To their credit, my family did everything they could to try and get him clean, but he died before what would have been his twenty-fifth birthday.

It was obvious that I was Doug's favorite child. I was the one who won all the awards, got into NYU, the one who became an Army Officer despite my rebellion and becoming a young single mother. I wasn't a particular fan of Doug's growing religious fervor, but because we still were close, I thought he would have my back no matter what, even if I hadn't followed the religious path that he had.

My parents were on and off toward the end of high school and divorced while I was at NYU. I was 100 percent put in the middle of the whole situation, and I took Doug's side. I cried and begged him not to do anything he would regret when on my last day of high school he left me a voice mail saying he was going to kill himself.

During college, he would call me, crying, at 2:00 a.m., and I would go into the stairwell of my freshman dorm to tell Doug it was going to be okay.

Eventually, he got together with his current wife, Donna, who was also deeply religious. I didn't care for her because Doug was wealthy, intelligent, and Donna was, well, a white trash West Virginian Doug had picked up on some Christian dating site. Even if she actually liked Doug, there was an obvious financial incentive there.

After having Lexi, I eventually warmed to Donna because someone gave me some advice early on: "You can't have too many people loving your kids." She seemed to care for my daughter, and that was good enough for me. As Doug became more religious, he became more controlling, to the point where numerous family members had witnessed Doug be verbally and emotionally abusive toward Donna. My own personal life was a mess around this time, and because I was so bonded with Doug, I think I turned a blind eye to this fact as well.

When I was married to Derek, he never cared for Doug. Whenever we had problems in our marriage, I ran to Doug, like I had always done throughout my life. If we needed money, I'd ask Doug. He always helped us, but now, in retrospect, I realize it was used as a method of control.

Years later, Derek told me that Doug was one of the (if not *the*) major contributing factors in our divorce.

I let Lexi stay with Doug and his wife, Donna, while I moved to Texas and got settled. I moved the summer right before Lexi's fourth grade year, during the peak of my struggle with PTSD, following the death of my brother, Derek, my husband, leaving me, and then Matty's murder.

Lexi had stayed with Doug and Donna a few times over the years when I would leave for military things, so I really didn't think much of it.

When Doug and Donna suggested Lexi stay through fifth grade, the rationale was that since all the kids would be new to the middle school in sixth grade, we might as well make it easier on Lexi until then, and that seemed perfectly reasonable to me.

Looking back, what a fool I was.

Doug had moved to what I can only describe as a compound in rural Virginia. He had become weirdly religious, but I noticed that it got worse after Thornton's death. He stopped celebrating Christmas. No church seemed to be good enough for him. At some point before Lexi moved there, Doug felt that God had come to him in his kitchen and told him that it was his mission to drive around to various churches around the country in an RV and tell them what they were doing wrong. I loved my dad, though, so I tried to dismiss him as quirky.

Since Thornton's death, Doug's behavior and religious extremism became markedly worse, but I didn't notice it until later since I didn't see him often enough to see the progression. Plus, I was blinded by dealing with my own problems.

In my defense, though, there was a moment I can point to that changed Doug from toxic to dangerous. About a week after Thornton's funeral in 2015, Doug was hiking his property in Virginia when he climbed into an old wooden deer stand to take a picture. The wood broke and Doug fell ten feet onto his head. Donna had to call EMS, and he had to be evacuated to a medical facility where it wasn't clear at first if he was going to make it. I am not a doctor, but I theorize that Doug possibly suffered a traumatic brain injury during that fall, which is why the worst parts of his personality became even more extreme after that year.

In May of 2018, when Doug suggested that Lexi continue to live with him, I said absolutely not. I told Doug I was grateful to him and Donna for their help, but I wanted my daughter back, *thank you very much*.

So when the time that Jason was supposed to arrive came and went, I had a panicked thought. Jason was approximately $10,000 behind in child support. Doug is extremely wealthy.

My gut told me my daughter was still in Virginia.

CHAPTER 16

Panic

I CALLED THE POLICE IN ALABAMA, WHERE JASON lived, I called the police in Round Rock, where I lived, and I called the police in Farmville, Virginia, where Doug lived. I called the FBI. I called the National Center for Missing and Exploited Children (NCMEC). I was a frantic mother in a race to get my daughter back.

I had a court order from Hawaii that gave me physical custody of Lexi. But behind my back, Doug had filed an emergency motion to grant himself custody of my daughter, and it was granted without so much as a notice to me.

When Doug found out I was getting law enforcement involved, he was not happy. He called me and threatened to tell not only Facebook about my involvement with Project Veritas but Google, where I currently worked, as well.

I had just begun instructor training at the dance studio, and the owners had said it would probably take a year until I had enough students for that to be my full-time job.

I worried that Doug's threats would not only jeopardize the work I had done investigating Facebook but that I would lose my current job at Google as well. So I contacted Brian (Joe Halderman's assistant at Project Veritas) to let him know what was going on.

I was already upset and frantic, but now, to add to it all, I was also mortified. The last thing I wanted was these people, whom I barely knew, to know about my family drama. I felt obligated to inform them, though, since Doug's interference could mess with their operations.

The police did nothing to help me, saying it was a civil matter, and the FBI never got back to me. The lawyer for the NCMEC was sympathetic but could only offer resources to give to the attorney I hired in Virginia.

One day, I got a menacing letter in the mail, allegedly from my daughter. It was a scrap of paper that had red marker aggressively scrawled on it saying how Jesus died for our sins and asking in all caps "WILL YOU ACCEPT HIM, CHRIST?"

There was no context to accompany it, but Doug clearly

had sent it to me since I recognized the handwriting on the envelope. The whole message was about death, and so I thought maybe Doug had finally lost it and went full Jim Jones. Early that morning, I remember being curled up in ball outside the Round Rock Police Department, begging for anyone to help me. A detective came out and began asking me about my own faith.

The absolute last thing I wanted to talk about was religion. My whole life, I had dealt with the more extreme versions of Christianity, and even though on an intellectual level, I can separate the religion itself from the worst parts of it, in practicality, I tend to stay as far away from it as humanly possible.

When the hearing date came, my lawyer and I thought it would be an open-and-shut case. I had a court order from Hawaii that had me as Lexi's primary guardian, and I had no accusations or history of abuse, neglect, or anything.

I underestimated how low Doug would sink. He dug up text messages from the worst days of my PTSD where I had panic attacks or a comment made about how I wanted to run my car into traffic. None of these were serious legitimate threats to my life, just a daughter venting to her father during a time when nothing seemed to be going right.

He tried to paint me as a party girl who associated with

criminals like Joe Halderman. He brought up my spotty job history, and I tried to explain that I was a corporate whistleblower and that was why I had lost my job. But of course, my findings hadn't been published yet, so the small-minded small-town judge looked at me like I was crazy.

At this time, I was still living on the poverty line and I certainly couldn't afford to fight a lengthy out-of-state legal battle against a multimillionaire. I was advised the best thing I could do was settle. I was so upset by the betrayal and the complete violation of trust that I honestly can't even remember signing the settlement. It was a deeply traumatic event—all I wanted was my baby girl back, whom I had raised mostly on my own since birth.

I argued that if I didn't have custody of Lexi, then Jason, her father, should. However, he was also being represented by Doug's attorney and voluntarily agreed to give up our daughter. I had begged him beforehand, in a text message, that even if he didn't agree with me, to get his own lawyer and not to be manipulated by Doug. Of course he didn't listen.

I was told that if I didn't sign the settlement, Doug would ruin my life. He would make accusations about my mental health that could affect my ability to get employment.

Completely bereft with grief, I sat in the car my mom had rented, outside the courthouse. I saw the "therapist," Beth Cook, give my father a high five outside the courtroom. Doug had hired her to make an assessment of my mental health despite never having spoken or interacted with me in any way. People were celebrating a child being taken away from their parents. Jason is an idiot and a jerk and he's done some *really* stupid things when it comes to our daughter, but I never called him unfit.

I saw my daughter outside the courtroom. She had been told that if she said she wanted to stay in Virginia, Doug would buy her a pony. I hopped out of the car and rushed to hug her and tell her goodbye. Through my sobs, I told her she would always be my daughter no matter what, that I would always love her no matter what, that she had done nothing wrong, and that I would always be there for her in any way that she needed.

After that, I didn't see or speak to my daughter for over a year.

CHAPTER 17

Becoming an Undercover Journalist

AUGUST, AUSTIN, TEXAS

AFTER THE MEETING IN JULY, KNOWING MY FINAN-cial situation, Brian suggested I do some contract work for Project Veritas. Now that I knew more about their current operations and what they were investigating, I had an idea to help with their *Deep State Investigation* series. I was incredibly grateful for the extra money, as now I had mounting legal bills since the fight for my daughter was just beginning. This meant that in total I was:

- Working full-time at the Google call center.
- Working what was essentially an apprenticeship

training program at the dance studio, for which I wasn't being paid.

- And now I was doing three days a week of contract work for Project Veritas.

Thankfully, they did not just throw me to the wolves on my first assignment.

I pulled up to Slab BBQ in North Austin. I had exchanged a few messages back and forth between the girl who was coming to help with the Austin Democratic Socialists of America (DSA) story, but I had no idea what she looked like, what her real name was, and so on.

She introduced herself using her code name: Liberty. I looked at her quizzically, but I wasn't terribly surprised that an organization like Project Veritas was weird about telling strangers their real names. She was petite and preppy looking and in a nice dress. Meanwhile, I was dressed in a *Game of Thrones*-themed basketball jersey and sweatpants because I was going to a hip-hop class later that evening.

At first, there was a lot of tension. She was clearly very leery of me.

We got our food and sat down, and at the table, she stopped to pray over her meal.

A little odd but okay.

Liberty proceeded to ask me about the Facebook story, what had happened, including the whole Ken situation. I knew she was asking me these questions in a specific way so she would appear friendly, but there was no denying that I was being interrogated. The questions came one after another, and I even offered her my phone to see some of the message traffic, although I had already shown it to James.

Once we started discussing the actual assignment, we knew the best thing to do would be to split up at the DSA meetings and act like we didn't know each other. I would feed her intel I got from my friend Jayden, who was in DSA, and she would go for the content. Since I had gotten into DSA through someone I had met from working at Google, I was there under my real name.

That's right. Technically, for two years (as of the time I'm writing this), I have been a card-carrying Democratic Socialist.

The first event Liberty and I went to was a speaking engagement they were hosting at a public library. I came armed with my hidden camera.

Despite wearing a camera during my time at Facebook,

it was still foreign and uncomfortable for me. There really is an art to it, and it's definitely a skill that has to be trained and honed over time. I was still a novice, so I would constantly fumble and bumble with the cameras, hyperaware of their presence but trying to convince myself that the people I was recording wouldn't be able to tell.

I set my camera apparatus (disguised as a common everyday object) down while I helped my "comrades" put away chairs and tables after the lecture. Yes, the DSA crowd unironically refer to each other as comrade.

After we finished, I left and got to my car before I realized I didn't have the camera.

I immediately went into a panic attack, thinking that it was going to be found by a DSA person who would quickly realize that it was not, in fact, the innocuous object it claimed to be but a hidden camera. I frantically started to search the room we had been in and the entryway of the library since they were closing.

Most of the DSA people had left, but Liberty was still outside. She could see me frantically searching while trying to look nonchalant. My first time out and I lost a camera. Remembering my days in the Army, my mind spiraled; I felt like such an idiot.

I'm sure I looked suspicious as all heck milling about. At one point, I broke the ruse and told Liberty, in a quick hushed tone as I passed by her, that I couldn't find my camera. I'm sure I looked crazed, and all I could think about was what a horrible first impression this was going to make and that I was never going to be able to work full time for Project Veritas.

For nearly an hour, I searched and scoured until the librarian kicked me out, saying they needed to close. At this point, I was relatively certain that all the DSA people had left.

I looked at the trash can sitting outside the library. Swallowing any sense of pride, I dived my hand in. The trash smelled of a mix of old liquids and bits of food that had been discarded over the course of the day. And there was a wetness to it. Finally, I felt what I had been looking for. The camera! It had been found!

I was so mortified about the experience that I didn't want to upload it to send to HQ. Luckily, we were not relying on the footage I was shooting.

Despite faking being a socialist, one positive thing to come out of the assignment was being social and making connections with the Austin DSA through people I had met during the course of my actual life. Luckily for me and my assignment, Jayden, my friend in the Austin DSA, used to work for the IRS, so he pointed out who the other government employees were.

Even though it was my first time, I will admit I had a hard time with this target. Jayden was someone I considered an actual friend. I didn't know he was in the DSA when we became friends because we would just talk about work and play video games. When he told me he was in the DSA, I invested more into the friendship, but we were genuinely close. When Lexi didn't come home, the tears I cried to him weren't fake. When he, another coworker, and I went to San Antonio for a Maroon 5 concert, I didn't have a camera, and I even invited him to come dancing with some of my friends. This is a perfect example of how undercover journalists like me don't hate or hold any personal animus toward the people we are investigating. Luckily, Jayden was just giving us the names of the DSA members who were still employees of the federal government, so that helped me justify the situation.

One day, Liberty was going to a potluck with her target, Thomas Sheehy. She was going to bake muffins, but her hotel didn't have an oven, so I opened up my home to her. This was maybe a week, if that, after the disastrous court hearing regarding my daughter.

While I cleaned my apartment in anticipation of Liberty

coming over, I picked up a photo of my daughter in a frame and started to cry. When I heard the knock at my door, I did my best to wipe away my tears. Although I had told Liberty about the situation, I didn't know her well enough to be vulnerable with her.

When I opened my front door, I was surprised to see Brian alongside Liberty, carrying a box with a massive arrangement of sunflowers.

Attached to the flowers was a note from James sending his sympathy for what had happened with my custody hearing. I still barely knew the man at the time, but it was a gesture that touched me. Brian and Liberty didn't know I had been crying right before they came, but the flowers and feeling like Project Veritas cared about the struggles I was going through personally reassured me I had made the right choice.

Liberty still needed some ingredients for the muffins, and since they arrived in an Uber, we jumped in my car and headed to a grocery store. I told her how much the flowers meant to me, and she told me she had worked for James for a few years and he was a very thoughtful person.

I had previously told Liberty all the same things I had told James and Brian during my trip to New York, but I mentioned that the flowers, and everything else with Project

Veritas, had reaffirmed the feelings I felt when I sent James an email shortly after being fired from Facebook.

I hadn't thought to include that particular email to help put together the Facebook story when I forwarded Brian old emails I had sent to Ken. It was meant to go to James, but Ken had informed me all communication was to go through him, and I had assumed he had forwarded the email. I never got a response, but I figured James was either busy or didn't care.

I pulled the email up on my phone and shared it with Liberty. Her eyes widened as she read it.

"I promise you, there is no way that James got this email," she told me resolutely.

"You think?"

"I definitely think you should send this to him again."

Here are parts of the actual email:

> Ken,
>
> We are having an ice storm today in Texas and so we're all homebound. As such, I had time to listen to the *entire* audiobook for American Pravda today.

To James (if you could pass the message along, nothing urgent so just when there's a free minute):

The book was wonderful. Not sure which one I like better, but I love that this one was available on Audible since you can hear the excitement come across in your voice during some of the higher-adrenaline moments.

I noted at the end you talked about being a despised person and how now in your early 30s it weighs on you. We are about the same age (I'm 31), and I wanted to say that I feel quite the opposite. The past three years of my life are something I would not have wished on my worst enemy. I've told a good bit of the story to Ken; maybe someday if we have the opportunity to meet, I can tell you the "it's so bad all I can do is laugh" truth of it all.

Without going into the gory details, life had left me at 31 feeling exhausted, jaded, and cynical about most things in the world. I knew *of* you, vaguely remembering the ACORN videos from when I was still in school. However, toward the end of the summer of 2016, I stumbled across the Project Veritas YouTube channel and ended up binge watching nearly the entire catalog in one night. Here were people pointing out the flaws in the system, often in an entertaining way. Lost in a period of career floundering after a car accident ended my military career, I thought, "I'd like to work with them" and applied to a Comms Director posting before the Rigging the Election series came out. I knew you were looking for insiders there, but as a content review agent in the intellectual property department, I didn't think I had anything of use to you until one day, I came across a copyright report from a conservative independent outlet and noticed some odd notes on the account. From there, I went down the proverbial rabbit hole and was appalled by the things I discovered.

I had left NYU as a freshman to join the Army thinking that was my way of making a difference in the world but was disappointed by the heavy levels of bureaucracy and grew cynical about my particular job being what I refer to as a "trained government mouthpiece."

After getting in touch with Ken, I was at first very hesitant. My job at Facebook was comfortable, there was free food, and it was by far the easiest job I had ever held. But as I dug deeper, I would look at the impact Project Veritas has made on the country (and with Silicon Valley, quite possibly the world) and realized that this was in fact my chance to do something that could *actually* make a difference. I felt reinvigorated and inspired, often staying up until the sun came up digging through thousands of internal pages, groups, and profiles.

Once I realized that the algorithm could tell I was looking at things, even if I never clicked on them, even if I was as careful as possible to browse in private mode, not to look at the full view of accounts if there was no associated ticket, etc., I knew I was playing a dangerous game. Supposedly, your tech guys know what/how they found things, but I realized that none of the messages were over SMS, always iMessage since they don't even show up on my phone bill, but it's possible when FB had me download beta clients for their products when I first started to work there, it put some sort of malware/monitoring software on my device.

Anyway, after the company wouldn't even let me go to my desk to get my personal belongings (which they still haven't returned, btw, not that there is anything "interesting" there except for some expensive headphones, some photos, and supplements), the first call I made after letting you and your team know what had happened was to my dad, a former attorney and one of the only people I had trusted with my secret. He asked me a simple question:

"Was it worth it?"

I paused only momentarily and answered yes. Admiration for you and the work of Project Veritas aside, the things I found the company doing were appalling and I felt the public had a right to know. PV just gave me the courage to do the right thing, even if it meant sacrificing my comfort.

Though you may be a reviled figure by those who are the

enemies of freedom, you have been for me personally a catalyst for change; an inspirational figure who brought back to life the little girl/teenager who was unafraid to take on institutions of power. The transformation has been physical and mental. It's actually very clear if you look at photos of me now vs even a year ago. You will never be reviled by me since you were instrumental in giving me my fire back. Your work has already made the world a better, more honest place, and your bravery and conviction are contagious.

Take a beat to enjoy the incredible accomplishments you and your team have made the past few weeks, have a fantastic book launch, and if there is anything else I can do to be of assistance, let me know. I haven't been able to contact the contract company yet, but all of my coworkers/immediate supervisors were shocked and confused by my sudden firing and they mentioned possibly being able to move me to a Google contract they have (which I'm skeptical of it working out, but wouldn't it be AMAZING if they did?!) since I was clearly so blindsided by the whole thing, but I handled the situation with a mixture of grace and ignorance, so they said they wanted to keep such an exemplary employee.

You'll always have an ally in me,

Cassandra Spencer

Very quickly, I got an email back from James asking if he could share the email with the rest of the company.

* * *

Especially going through my custody battle, James would often remind me of this quote by Martin Luther King Jr.: "The arc of the moral universe is long, but it bends towards justice."

For so long, I felt like I had always tried to do the "right" thing but that no one recognized it or cared.

That email, not seen until seven months after it was originally written, was a crucial turning point in my relationship with James. He finally understood why I felt so passionately about doing what I did, even if it had meant losing everything in the process.

When the *Deep State Investigation* series released in the fall of 2018, ending with the footage that Liberty obtained of Thomas Sheehy discussing how he would do DSA work on government time, or how he couldn't "technically" violate the Constitution of the United States, I was flown back to New York. This time, instead of being regarded with suspicion by the people in the office, I felt welcomed and embraced. It was my first time meeting and interacting with the other journalists, and they all thought what I had done was amazing.

I remember everyone excitedly watching the TV as our stories were commented on by Mike Pompeo, the Secretary of State. The work, which as small as my part was in it, was making an impact. Several government employees were forced to resign, and investigations had been opened into the DSA's use of government resources against political opponents. The feeling gave me life. My whole life, I had wanted to make an impact on the world, and through Project Veritas, I felt like I was finally getting my chance.

And since it was the fall of 2018 and we were hitting peak election season, we hadn't even released the Facebook story yet.

CHAPTER 18

Through the Looking Glass

I FLEW BACK TO AUSTIN FROM NEW YORK ON A high. I was so happy and excited about what I had accomplished on my first undercover assignment, but I couldn't really tell anybody.

In fact the next day, I was back in the cubicle farm, taking customer service calls for YouTube TV as a Google contractor. I still hated the job, but my plan had been to stick with it until teaching dance could become my full-time vocation since that would be the best plan once Lexi was home with me full time.

I started to work more with Project Veritas because I had the time since Lexi wasn't home, and I found that working excessively kept me from falling off the cliff into a pit of depression. So by September, I worked full time as a Google contractor, worked part time as a Project Veritas contractor, trained to be a dance instructor, and also prepared for dance competitions with my dance pro, David.

Because I worked full time and oftentimes switched to a Project Veritas assignment immediately after my shift at Google, my private dance lesson weren't until 9:30 p.m. Moderation has never been something I've been good at, and although spinning all the plates kept me from lying in bed and crying nonstop over the loss of my daughter, something was bound to eventually crash.

One night during my dance lesson, I kept doing something incorrectly. I was not mentally there, hadn't been practicing, and David who was so patient when I first learned to dance (literally dragging me in a circle on the floor) and who threw me into the deep end of the pool when he had me perform in front of people after only a couple of months of lessons, had had enough.

I can't even remember what it was exactly, but something set him off.

"I can't do this. *You* can't keep doing this," he said. "You are stretched *way* too thin, and you can't do anything properly. Something has got to give. You've got way too much on your plate. If you keep this up, you *will* be in last place."

I had a competition coming up soon, and I knew he was right.

I kept it together until I got to my car, where I broke down sobbing. I was upset that I had pushed David to that point of frustration. As hurt and embarrassed and upset as I was, he was right. I couldn't keep doing things the way I had been. Initially, I didn't want to be a full-time journalist because the travel required wasn't conducive to having my daughter home with me. But since Lexi wasn't with me and I was burning myself out, something needed to change.

The following day, I called Brian and gave Project Veritas an ultimatum: either I needed to make Project Veritas my primary job so I could quit the call center, or I was done.

I had a formal offer letter within two days.

Not only was I excited to work for Project Veritas full time, but deeper down inside, it also gave me satisfaction regarding my struggles with my father.

Although I don't have a formal diagnosis, in my thirties, it has been heavily speculated by several psychiatrists, therapists, and others that I am on the autism spectrum, which actually makes a lot of sense. For example, when I get excited about or interested in something, it becomes all I want to talk about. When I was still working at Facebook, before our falling out, I had told Doug about Ken and how inspiring James was to me. I told him everything. Over Thanksgiving the year prior, when I wouldn't shut up about how amazing and what an inspiration James and Project Veritas were, he'd quickly shut me down. "Give it up, Cassandra. You will never work at Project Veritas, and James O'Keefe will never know who you are. This is just like you with the Backstreet Boys."

The cliché goes that hindsight is twenty-twenty and that's true with Doug. Doug tried to paint me in court as a loser who never amounted to anything. And even though his lies there seemed like such a punch to the gut, the fact is, he never really believed in me.

After the custody battle, the little girl within me, who always looked for validation, worried he was right. When I sent in that signed offer letter, however, there was a satisfaction in knowing I had proved him wrong.

And now that I had nothing else to focus on, I was going to prove him wrong even more.

CHAPTER 19

Beto O'Rourke

WITHIN DAYS OF MY START DATE WITH PROJECT Veritas, I was on a plane to El Paso. I was assigned to the Beto O'Rourke campaign, probably since I already lived in Texas. It was already October, so I was getting a late start; other journalists had been in senate campaigns around the country for months prior, and I had less than one month.

All the hemming and hawing about Project Veritas tricking people into saying things is 100 percent false. Unsurprisingly, being an undercover journalist is very similar to being a conventional journalist.

And before any recent journalism school (J-School) graduate points out that I have never worked as a journalist, I will remind you that I served as a Public Affairs Officer in the Army for a large portion of my adult life and I have been through a significant amount of journalism training, even though I never worked for a traditional news organization.

A Project Veritas undercover journalist is the same as a conventional journalist in the sense that they simply ask questions or bring up topics of conversation. To the political operatives, who I'm sure are reading this book in hopes of gaining some kind of silver bullet to try and prevent themselves from being the subject of a Project Veritas exposé, here's the answer:

> Be honest, be transparent, and don't do anything illegal or unethical.

I know those are crazy ideas in politics, but the truth is (and I almost have to laugh at how simple it really is) that if people acted in that manner, as a journalist, I would walk away with nothing, and the campaign would have had a very hardworking volunteer in their offices for a while.

I became close with the field manager, Dominic Chacon, as well as several other staffers in the office during the month I was there. I worked in the office doing routine campaign tasks, such as phone banking, and would volunteer for extra assignments, such as putting kits together for field offices. I tried to be as friendly and personable as possible and, most importantly, try to listen to everything going on.

The 2018 Texas senate race between Beto O'Rourke and Ted Cruz was a close one. The Beto campaign saw it as an important opportunity to turn Texas blue.

One of the advantages of having grown up in a place like Hawaii, which is far left, and attending schools like NYU, which is also far left, is that not only did I feel firm in my beliefs, having had them challenged at every turn in my life, but I also understood how people like those who worked on the Beto campaign thought. As anyone who spent time doing debate team in high school or college can tell you, it is an incredibly valuable intellectual exercise to try and argue not only the position that you actually advocate for on any side of an argument but the opposing position as well. Regardless of whether you are an undercover journalist or someone who likes to talk about politics on Facebook, having the mental elasticity to think like the other person not only makes you better in a debate, but it also tends to give you empathy for them as an individual and not view them as evil or disturbed, which very few people actually are.

I would say the majority of people I met during the course of my tenure as an undercover journalist were not inherently bad people. This doesn't excuse any of the things they did or said, but decent people, especially when put in a position of political power (or who are vying for a position of political power), can and do bad things.

That late October was one of those examples. During this time, the Honduran migrant caravan was a hot topic in the news. I had been in the office and it was getting late, probably close to 9:00 p.m., and I was getting ready to call it a day and head back to my hotel. Suddenly, one of the staffers got a phone call and said that some of the migrants had arrived early, and there were hundreds of them staying in an El Paso church.

The video is available on the Project Veritas Action channel, but when you hear me sound surprised at the events, that isn't Oscar-worthy acting on my part. That is a genuine reaction. I did not know this was going to happen.

The staffers had often talked about how "Daddy Beto" would freely hand out prepaid credit cards to be used for the campaign. That campaign had raised more money than any in senate campaign history, and they were flush with cash.

As the field manager, Dominic was in charge of about a dozen field organizers. He reached out to all of them and said we were going to use the campaign money to buy food and other resources for the migrants. He talked about the excuses he could make up if anyone ever found out or questioned the expenditures.

"We'll just say it was for block walkers."

"For the fruit, we'll just tell them we wanted a really healthy breakfast!"

"To hide the rice, we'll just say that someone was making arroz con leche."

Because I had become friendly with them, when one of the field organizers asked me if I wanted to go to the store with her to help her get all the supplies, I quickly accepted. I felt my heart start to pound. I wasn't sure what the story would be when I was first assigned to this investigation—being the first of my Project Veritas career—but the second this happened, I knew this was it.

Of course, I wasn't prepared for this moment. Not only were the memory cards I had almost full, but the camera batteries I was using were almost dead. I had been in the field all day and had no clue that something like this was going to happen in the middle of the night.

I ducked outside for a moment and frantically began to message HQ. Everyone was excited.

Back inside, we made a plan of all the supplies we were going to get. Things like food and even first aid and hygiene supplies would be easy enough to justify as legitimate campaign spending, but things like clothes and blankets?

They had a solution for this: it was to climb into the curbside donation bins used by the Salvation Army and other thrift stores and take things from there.

"If I have to climb into essentially a dumpster for this job," I remember thinking to myself. No one said life as an investigative journalist was going to be glamorous.

As the shopping expedition was happening, I could feel my work phone going off with my supervisor, Elton, and James wanting to know the updates on the caper. I couldn't respond and was doing everything I could to conserve battery life to be sure that the whole experience was caught on film.

We bought so much at the grocery store that the field organizer's, Anapaula Theman's, car, which I was riding in, was completely full. She still had me keep a lookout for any of the Salvation Army and Goodwill donation bins on the street corners. When we didn't come across any, I was secretly relieved.

"I hope the wrong person doesn't find out about this,"

Anapaula said to me as we drove toward the church where the migrants were staying.

"If only you knew," I silently thought to myself.

When I finally made it back to my hotel, James wanted to call me right away. Despite the fact it was probably 2:00 a.m. on the East Coast, he wanted to hear about my experience. I was exhausted, exhilarated, and still a little bit in shock at what I had witnessed. The Beto O'Rourke campaign had clearly used campaign funds to buy supplies for people who were in the country illegally, while trying to hide it as supplies they were buying for campaign volunteers. In addition to basic supplies such as food, water, and medical supplies, the campaign arranged to use campaign vehicles to give the migrants rides to airports and bus stations, and they were supposed to return to El Paso at some point for immigration hearings as part of the "catch and release" program happening during that time. And this was just one night in El Paso—hundreds of migrants would flood the country in the meantime. This underscored the problem the United States had with mass uncontrolled migration. Even though there was still more work to be done, I knew I had a story on my hands.

The next day, I was on a plane back home to Austin for a couple of days because I was trying to hold on to some shred of my real life at the dance studio. I still had dance competitions I had committed to before I signed up to work full time at Project Veritas.

Working for Beto's campaign was my first official experience working undercover, and it was strange to me how after only a few weeks, I quickly got used to hearing the name I was using (Jennifer) and how foreign my own name sounded. Seeing David and the other people in my life was a relief. It felt like, for at least a moment, I could set my feet back on the ground before being swept off into Veritas world again.

When I arrived back in El Paso, it was straight to work. It wasn't enough to only have the events that unfolded the previous night on film. We wanted to get as much corroboration as possible that not only did the events I had been witness to take place but that the entire campaign staff, not just those at the ground level, were perfectly aware and even supportive of it.

On Halloween, I knocked on doors at a residence in El Paso. Beto O'Rourke's wife, Amy Hoover Sanders, was there to serve as motivation to help the volunteers cross the finish line off her husband's campaign. When everyone was dividing up what streets they were going to go knock doors on, I genuinely had to stifle a smile and a small laugh when Amy and her brother-in-law said they were going to knock doors on O'Keefe Drive.

Talk about foreshadowing.

I was working in the field on this story literally until the release, which was three days before the election. My last morning going into the campaign office, I talked to the campaign manager, Jody Casey, during breakfast. At the same time, James had flown down from the Project Veritas offices in New York and was out filming the narration that would set the scene for the public of the undercover footage I recorded.

When I saw James and the crew that was with him from the office, I remember breathing a huge sigh of relief. Even though I had gone home and had a brief reprieve from my double life, it's not like I freely told people in Austin what I did for a living. The people at Project Veritas were the only ones who really knew what I had been up to for the past few weeks, and seeing them and having people congratulate me on the great job I had done was the validation I had needed.

Within the first month of my employment at Project Veritas, I had managed to uncover potential campaign finance violations as well as a blatant attempt by the Beto campaign to cover up the activity, merely days before the 2018 midterm elections.

The story blew up immediately. All the local stations in

Texas were forced to cover it, it garnered a comment from both Beto and his opponent, Ted Cruz, and in addition to millions of online views, made several national media outlets.

Until then, there was always a slight fear that I had only been given my job out of pity for how much I had struggled after everything that had happened at Facebook. By getting my first real story, I had justified my hiring.

After the whirlwind of activity in El Paso, I was about to fly back to Austin to get working on my next assignment, and the rest of the team was going back to New York. Elton had told me to avoid being seen in public with James since exposing my identity could mean the end of my undercover career. So when the rest of the team went to return the rental car, I split off from James immediately. I was checking my phone, so I was startled when someone embraced me.

"Thank you. I feel very strongly about you and what you've done," James said to me before walking away to his gate.

In that moment, my brain confirmed what my gut had told me back in July. Ken had lied, James was not a cold, calculating narcissist, and he was, in fact, a good person. I had made the right choice in trusting him.

Even more so than the comment from James, though, I was touched by an unexpected call from Joe Halderman, who I knew was, in addition to the scandal that took him out of the news industry, an eight-time Emmy winner and was nominated for an Oscar for his news work.

I remember getting the call from him in the last moments before the flight attendant made sure all phones were switched to airplane mode.

"I just wanted to tell you that you did a great job, and it's a pleasure working with you."

The validation I got internally, the millions of views and millions of dollars of earned media the story gained externally, validated that I was no pity hire. I was now a full-time journalist, and I told myself I was going to be as good at it as I could possibly be.

CHAPTER 20

The Girl with the Pink Hair

OUR OBJECTIVE FOR 2019 WAS CLEAR: EXPOSE BIG Tech. We were going to tell my Facebook story, but that was only meant to be the beginning. This story was going to inspire other insiders from Facebook and other companies to come forward and tell their stories.

I can't tell you how many meetings I attended to go over "the documents," which ended up being around fifty pages of internal postings from Facebook, including for the first time, thanks to the screenshots and video stills I had from working on various accounts, a peak of what the back end of people's pages and profiles actually looked like.

I spent the beginning of 2019 living out of a hotel in San

Francisco to be closer to the tech companies, specifically Facebook, Google, and Twitter. The first three months of the year were spent trying to meet people who worked for these companies. It wasn't hard for me to make friends with them since as a slightly awkward nerdy half Asian, I fit right in.

Although I won't go into the specifics of what I did to meet people, I will say it's not entirely unlike what you would normally do if you moved to a new city where you don't know anybody. However, as a pretty extreme introvert, I was suddenly forced to become a social butterfly on steroids, which made for interesting but extremely exhausting days.

In places like San Francisco, sometimes the best way to fit in is to be outlandish, so I dyed my hair bright pink. I took dance lessons when I was in the area and even found a gay country western dance hall to go to.

I had an Instagram account, where I posted pictures of my adventures around the city hanging out in Japantown and did my best to make as many connections as possible.

One time, I remember a girl from Twitter telling me two of her coworkers were looking for a third roommate and she thought I'd be perfect. There was no way I would have been able to do that, legally or ethically, due to California's recording laws as well as Project Veritas's standards, but I remember telling my colleagues, "But imagine if I *could!*"

Much of the time, being an undercover journalist was like being the ultimate method actor. I had my alias down. I could have easily answered any questions about her life, and I spent weeks living my life as "Christina," which was the name I was using on this particular assignment.

Other times, though, it was more like being a private investigator. Aside from making connections, my colleagues and I needed to track down the specific engineers who were the architects for the deboost code and the authors of the *Troll Report* so James could ask them questions and confront them about their work.

The deboost code was what started me down this whole rabbit hole—the code I had noticed only on prominent conservative pages during my time at Facebook. The *Troll Report* discussed how Facebook wanted to address "trolling" on its platform, but it became quite clear after reading the document that it was targeted at right-wingers. We wanted to know who the human beings influencing the censoring practices at Facebook were because it is one thing to shout endlessly at a corporation about censorship, but it is much more impactful to confront the people responsible for it and simply ask them to explain themselves.

One slide described troll behavior on Facebook to include "red-pilling normies to convert them to their worldview," and the example video was a link to a YouTube video *The-Blaze* personality, Lauren Chen, titled "Why Social Justice Is Cancer."

The *Troll Report* went on to describe how their algorithms already demoted and removed "bad" content, but they wanted to take it even further.

They created a list of features that they wanted to implement. One of these included notifying a user's friends and family if they had been suspended for posting something that violated the community guidelines.

Another was assigning a "troll score" to all accounts to determine the likelihood they were a troll. This worked similar to another tool that they had called the Fake Account Index, where a numerical score was assigned to an account based off the types of posts, if they were friends with other accounts that had been flagged as fake, as well as other behaviors. If a profile's score was above a certain threshold, the account was deemed as fake and taken down.

Once this happens to a user, it is damn near impossible to get off it even if you know someone at the company!

True story. My grandmother's ninety-year-old sister was

flagged as a fake account and was banned from Facebook. Worried, my grandmother called me and asked if there was anything I could do since Facebook was this woman's only real outlet. I'm sure she posted the same spammy memes we see elderly people post all the time—most of it you scroll past and move on.

When she tried to appeal the ban, Facebook asked her to provide a copy of her driver's license, which she did. They still refused to overturn it.

Since this was someone I personally knew and I was working at Facebook at the time, I submitted a ticket to the appropriate team to ask they reinstate her account. After a couple of days, they did, and my grandmother called me overjoyed and so thankful that I had helped out her sister.

A couple of days later, they reinstated the ban despite having a copy of this woman's driver's license and personal reassurance from someone at the company that the account was, in fact, for a real person.

Think about this the next time Facebook tries to explain away mass bans as Russian troll farms. Although there is certainly a problem with people creating fake accounts for the sole purpose of causing chaos on the platform, I cannot think of (nor did I ever receive) a single good reason as to why this ninety-year-old woman was banned despite having heaps of evidence to verify she was a real person, one who posted a few too many memes with teddy bears and sparkles on them.

This troll score would seek to work in a similar way to the Fake Account Index, judging the likelihood that a user was a troll based on who their friends were, what groups they were a part of, memes they had posted, and words they would use in their posts.

The terms that would label one as a troll were clearly aimed at the 4chan and meme culture that had been appropriated by the right to help Donald Trump win the 2016 election. Some of the terms identified included *lulz*, *normie*, *sjw* (social justice warrior), and *MSM* (a common acronym for mainstream media).

We already knew when we planned to release the documents and launch the "Be Brave" campaign, where we put out the call for whistleblowers from all walks of life, from Big Tech to media and beyond, to reach out to Project Veritas, that a large portion of the piece was going to be interviewed in silhouette.

One night late in my hotel room, I was getting ready to wind down when I received a call from James. He had a plan that at the Conservative Political Action Conference (CPAC), which was happening shortly after the anticipated release date, we would unveil my identity to the world.

"I know I'm essentially asking you to become a public figure," James said (by this point, he knew I was someone who considered herself an awkward nerd).

"I mean, whatever is going to make the piece more impactful."

"Well, I know that's a lot to consider, so sleep on it."

I knew that my evidence alone wasn't going to be the sole thing that caused any actual change or reform to happen in the Big Tech and social media space. We were going to need more whistleblowers, and considering I was the first, there was a part of me that was skeptical as to how many more would actually come forward.

My biggest thing was that I didn't want all the sacrifices I had made, the humiliation of my firing, the loss of a potential career, the court battle where I was made to look crazy, to be for nothing. If that meant getting up on stage to encourage other whistleblowers, I was ready and willing to do so.

When the day came for us to shoot the interview, I thought, *Oh, I'm going to be blacked out so no one will see me*, so I dressed more or less like a bum that day. I had no makeup on and threw on a Sailor Moon denim jacket.

So when the production crew wanted to shoot a series of establishing and b-roll shots of James and me walking from behind, both at the interview location and around San Francisco, I regretted my wardrobe decisions. *I really wish I had worn something else today*, I thought to myself.

James had prepped me for the interview. In his mind, he wanted it to be like the *60 Minutes* interview with Edward Snowden. The whole experience of having James interview a subject who was intentionally sitting down for an interview, rather than confronting one who had been caught on undercover video, was new to both of us, and we were nervous.

I had told the story so many times at that point that I think there was a part of me in the moment that was a little numb. The bulk of the interview was spent talking about the evidence we uncovered, but toward the end, we talked about getting fired and locked in a room and how they tried to demand to see my personal phone. We also talked about the conversation I had with my (now estranged) father to tell him that I thought it was 100 percent worth it despite being thrust into poverty and applying for food stamps to survive, and so on.

We took a break at one point, and James told me, "It's okay if you cry."

I had been preparing for this interview mentally for so long that I didn't feel a whole lot when I was talking. In fact, it felt more awkward at first telling James the same story I had told him what felt like a million times over already.

When we wrapped on the filming, I went to the green room of the place we had rented and lay down on the couch. Suddenly, all the emotions I had repressed came to the surface. I bawled.

The main thing I thought of was my daughter, hoping that someday, she would know the story of this journey and be proud of who her mother was. I had been painted by Doug to be a mentally unstable party girl, which to anyone who knew me was laughable, but I could see the years of brainwashing were already affecting her.

The pain of not even being able to see my daughter and knowing that she was being raised in an environment that was horrible for her continued to wear on me.

The interview wasn't the end of our day, though. We still had engineers to confront.

Tracking those engineers down involved finding out where they lived, where they worked, and what their schedules and habits were like so that we could either befriend them or, as the case ended up being, simply confront them with their own work to question them about it.

Watching the people who are caught on tape (or in this case, on paper) be confronted is still probably the most exhilarating experience at Project Veritas. Occasionally, you have a subject who is actually reflective on what they've said, but most of the time, they just refuse to talk and run away.

Danny Ben David and Seiji Yamamoto were no different. We caught them both during their morning commutes to the Facebook Menlo Park campus. James literally walked up to them with the work they had produced, with their names on it, and they froze and refused to say anything about it. Yamamoto actually claimed to be in fear of his safety and rode away on a bike so quickly the chain skipped.

Project Veritas has one of the hardest working production teams in the business because less than twenty-four hours later, the story was released.

We spent one day at HQ in New York before going to CPAC.

I would also like to take this opportunity to address one of the more popular things people commented on my video—that I was going to be recognized by Facebook because of my pink hair:

1. At the time of the release, it had already been a year since I left Facebook, so it wouldn't have mattered.
2. Within forty-eight hours of my shooting that interview, I was in a salon chair going from pink to blond so that I wouldn't be easily recognizable at CPAC.

Being at CPAC for the first time was like entering another world. I was so used to being completely surrounded by and immersed with people from the left that I actually felt incredibly awkward and out of place. I had bought dresses specifically to wear to the event, and my heels were actually my practice heels for dance since they were comfortable and broken in.

I still wasn't sure whether I were going to go public or not. On the one hand, it would be great to tell my story and I wasn't afraid of the media. On the other hand, once I was public, my ability to work as an undercover journalist would be seriously hindered. Elton was against the idea because he wanted to keep me in the field.

Another reason CPAC was different was because even though I knew James was a public figure, it had never been an issue throughout the duration of my friendship with him.

At CPAC, however, James was routinely swarmed by young college students and other supporters who wanted autographs and selfies. I will never forget when we arrived at the hotel in the middle of the night, bleary eyed and tired because we had been going nonstop since we filmed the interview in San Francisco a couple of days prior, we got in the elevator to go to our respective rooms. A woman in the elevator with us immediately recognized James and began to gush about both *Breakthrough* and *American Pravda*.

I stayed silent and watched the numbers slowly beep as we went up the elevator floor by floor. Suddenly, the woman turned to me, shocked I had no reaction to being in an elevator with James O'Keefe, and said, "Do you know who this man is?"

I quietly nodded, desperate to get to my room because I probably hadn't slept for two days at that point.

As much as I wanted to check out the event, I still had the neon pink hair I had in the Facebook video, so I instead spent more than eight hours at the hairdresser getting every trace of the color out of my hair, which left me as a light blonde. When I stopped by a hotel room where the team had congregated, James turned to me and almost didn't recognize me for a second.

"Your hair...it's not...weird anymore."

"Thank you, James—what every woman wants to hear." I laughed.

The organizers of CPAC were understanding of my situation, but they needed to see my real driver's license for security, which I happily showed them. They did meet me in the middle, though, and my ID badge for the weekend said, "Corgi Smith—Project Veritas."

Admittedly, I was a little overwhelmed by the whole event, and to avoid clinging to James like a child about to be lost at the department store, my best friend, Jessica, attended the event with me. We listened to a few speeches, including a fiery one by Michelle Malkin that still resonates with me to this day.

I had been hanging toward the back of the room, but right before James's speech, one of the event organizers rushed to find me and sat me in the front row. It was a great speech. He did a good job explaining some of the more technical aspects of what I had found, and I saw my photo, in silhouette, up on the massive screens.

"Listen, it takes enormous moxie to do what she did, all right? She lost her job for giving us documents and she went on food stamps for six months."

I remember turning red in my seat and wanting to bury

my face in my hands. Yes, I did go on food stamps after I got fired from Facebook and it was the most humiliating thing I had ever done. All through college, I had made it as a single mom without needing help from the government. However, I realized that in that exact moment, I knew it was a temporary stopgap and I was not in a position to let my pride overrule my need to eat.

For some reason, the food stamp thing would come up in every interview, and I remember pleading with James, "Can we *please* stop mentioning the food stamps?" At that point, it had almost become a joke. The speech carried on.

"I asked her, 'Was it worth it?' and she said, 'Yes,' and I said, 'Why?' and she said, 'Because I found what the company was doing was so appalling that I felt the public had a right to know. So she lost her job. I believe she's here today. I can't point her out, for obvious reasons, but she's actually sitting somewhere in the front row!"

He said this while intentionally looking out in another direction from where I was sitting so as to not draw attention to me. People around me began to applaud and stand, and eventually, the whole room was on their feet.

That was an awkward moment for me because I obviously knew the applause was for me, but it felt egotistical and wrong to applaud myself. My identity was still a secret, though, so if I didn't stand up and clap, it would be obvious that it was me. I stood up and very awkwardly clapped for myself. Regardless, it was a good feeling to know there were people out there who supported me and what I had done.

Once the applause died down, James continued with his speech: "Here's the bottom line: I asked her, 'Was it worth it?' She said, 'Yes, because the public had a right to know,' but she basically said on condition that 'more people do what I do.'"

Immediately after his speech, Cary Poarch, who would go on to be the CNN insider who would record hundreds of hours of hidden video and audio within the media conglomerate, approached James at the book signing he held immediately afterward.

The plan had worked, and people began to come forward to Project Veritas with their stories.

CHAPTER 21

Julian Assange

APRIL 11, 2019, 5:30 A.M.
ROUND ROCK, TEXAS

"ASSANGE GOT ARRESTED," A COLLEAGUE POSTED in a group chat.

As a former military officer, one who held a TS/SCI clearance (above Top Secret for those not familiar with the terms), I had mixed feelings. When I was a young lieutenant, I remember incidentally being at Fort Meade during Chelsea Manning's trial. That was in 2012, and I had been an officer for a year and a half, working in the intelligence field. Wikileaks has always been a confusing topic for me on an emotional gut level.

For the record, let me be clear. I think what Chelsea

Manning did was wrong. I think Manning was a terrible soldier and a deeply troubled human being prior to leaking classified information. Her record included reports of punching a female officer prior to transitioning from Bradley to Chelsea.

But how do I reconcile a strong dislike of Manning and a general mixed bag of feelings toward Assange and Wikileaks with my current vocation and my actions as a corporate whistleblower?

I jotted a quick response in the group chat but deleted it after a few minutes. It was far too early in the morning to be having an existential crisis.

People often liken Project Veritas to political hit men, but I can say with 100 percent certainty that was never the case for me or anyone I knew.

One thing that people would be surprised to know is how much ideological diversity there is at Project Veritas. There were people from all over the spectrum, from deeply religious conservatives such as my best friend at work, "Bri," to hard-core libertarians, to people who would have been considered liberals in the '90s.

The goal of the Project Veritas journalist, as we were constantly reminded, was to "expose the devil"—to expose the lying, the corruption, the hypocrisy. It was always about the story and not "we need to get something on X person."

Being around people whom you can disagree with but still care about is something that seems to have gotten lost in American political discourse. I felt grateful to have it at Project Veritas. This was an instance where I had to challenge my own long-held belief that Julian Assange equals bad. He was bad because in the Army, I was taught that leaks were a horrible, awful thing that had to be stopped at all costs and that they were a massive threat to our national defense.

My own actions, if I continued to hold such a black-and-white view of the situation, would mean I was a bad person for leaking the documents related to Facebook. I knew I had done the right thing though, so I begrudgingly began to take a more nuanced stance on people like Julian Assange.

That was one thing I always appreciated about the job. The intellectual challenge, the discussions of ethics, and how you could have a disagreement (in some cases, a heated one) with a colleague but still work together toward a common purpose.

The whole crew felt like a family to me, especially since I

was so estranged from my own. When I went to company-wide meetings in the past, I would roll my eyes and drag my feet with dread, but I found myself looking forward to seeing my colleagues who were working on their own investigations around the country.

My other home was back in Austin, and I looked forward to those visits as well. Even though I was no longer training to be a dance instructor, I continued to use dance as an outlet and escape, both in and out of the field. Most of the time, it was kind of amusing and fun for me to have this strange double life.

Other times, it was just work. Hard work.

To any aspiring journalists out there reading this, I would 110 percent recommend working for Project Veritas. It will be some of the most rewarding work you will ever do, and you will work alongside some of the best people you will ever meet.

But living out of a suitcase, being home only a couple of days a month, and oftentimes being completely alone in a hotel far away from friends and family gets lonely.

I was working on multiple investigations, but by the summer, it was time to start thinking about the 2020 election and the democratic primaries. Cities in Iowa are small, so we had to be extra cautious when out in the field. I remember gaining weight during that summer because I was so tired that the only refuge I found was in the Red Lobster I had delivered to my hotel room.

I began to have an especially hard time because my daughter's birthday is in June, so not being able to see or talk to her was weighing heavily on me. The only contact I had during that time was through postcards I sent to her from each city I visited, but I was never sure if the letters and cards would make it to her past Doug. James and the Project Veritas team knew how much the situation with my daughter weighed on my heart. Elton had children himself, and during that summer, I found myself crying to him on the phone on more than one occasion.

I wanted to be someone my daughter could be proud of, and I didn't want the time spent away from her to be for nothing, so I continued to grind at my job.

Just like at Facebook when I reached a point where I could no longer stand on the sidelines and do nothing, despite the previous defeat and knowing that I was putting myself back into a traumatic situation, I had to try and save my daughter. I used the small amount of money I had managed to save and put it toward fighting to get Lexi back.

CHAPTER 22

Making an Impact

JUNE 11, 2019, 11:46 P.M.
DES MOINES, IOWA

"I HOPE YOU'RE SEEING THE FRUITS OF YOUR LABOR,"
James said to me via text.

My work phone dinged after a long day of going from
campaign event to campaign event, trying to see if there
was a story surrounding the 2020 Democratic primary
election. I had a long day that involved spending several
hours driving around rural Iowa and an awkward encoun-
ter where I had to hold former Vice President Joe Biden's
hand for two to three minutes.

The life of a Project Veritas journalist.

Earlier that day, Project Veritas had launched a video. Another tech insider, this time from Pinterest, had come forward. I had watched the story in the morning and was amazed at how nefarious even a company like Pinterest, to which my shock was even up as a potential story, was acting behind closed doors. Pinterest, the website my ex-husband and I used to pin home DIY projects for our couples blog.

I watched the story in the morning but had pushed it to the side in my mind to focus on my task at hand. So I didn't know what James was talking about at first.

"What do you mean, in Iowa?" After all, it was nearly midnight for me, 1:00 a.m. in New York, and here was my boss, texting me.

He flooded my messages with some of the media headlines.

"This was inspired by what you did."

"You caused this."

James knows that I'm generally not one to seek out the spotlight. I humbly said I just hope my story helped to encourage others to come forward.

"You were the spark."

"Don't ever forget that when you're feeling down."

Earlier that day, I had whined to my immediate supervisor, Elton, that I was feeling burned out after spending nearly a month on the road and working weeks without a day off.

"Can I please go home? I'm just asking for *one* day."

"No, I hear you, but we need you out in the field," Elton told me.

I grumbled about it on my way to my events that day and sulked like a sullen teenager in my hotel room.

After hearing our Pinterest insider had been fired, I put my own woes aside and wrote out a short note that I wasn't sure if I should send or not—just a friendly "be brave, hang in there" sort of thing, as someone who had also been fired from a Big Tech company.

James responded that he was on his way to pick up Eric from the airport and asked if I would still be awake to talk to him.

Knowing what a stressful and confusing time it can be immediately after being fired, I kept the conversation pretty lighthearted, comparing and laughing over our two stories of being unceremoniously ousted from our workplaces. I did give him one warning:

"I'm sorry, but the food at the tech companies is better. That's the one thing I miss the most."

CHAPTER 23

Releasing Jen Gennai

FOR THE NEXT FEW DAYS, I CONTINUED IN IOWA until I was so frustrated that I took to passive-aggressively sending Elton videos of the Blake Shelton song "Home."

It would have been bad enough had I just been working for three weeks. But aside from taking on Big Tech, voter fraud, and crooked politicians, I had been training for another mission.

I was doing a dance competition in South Korea, and I was scheduled to leave in a couple of days, but my current work timeline didn't even give me enough time to get home and clean my costumes, let alone work with my coach or practice.

So I did what any other rational, thirty-two-year-old adult would do: I started crying. Literally crying. I was despondent, and my coworkers had to drag me out of my room to have dinner while I was having a meltdown.

Over the course of those last few miserable days in Iowa, I had been told frequently, "Content is your ticket home."

"I gave you content from Google, but for some bizarre reason, you're not publishing it."

I repeated this same conversation with Elton every night.

One thing my parents scolded me about when I was a kid was my incessant need to whine. Frequently and loudly.

Well, little did I know the snowball effect that whining would have.

The following morning, I was on a flight back home to Austin.

After the week I had and the tug-of-war with leadership, when my work phone lit up with "JO" literally as the plane landed, I rolled my eyes and groaned. I thought to myself, *What now? Can't you leave me alone for one freaking day?*

Putting on my best phone voice, I answered, "Hello?"

"I have good news for you. We're publishing the Google story."

"Wait. What?"

"We were already going to publish, but as we were working on it, an insider came forward and is willing to go on camera. He's flying out tonight."

My eyes welled up with tears. "I'm crying again, but it's happy crying this time."

James laughed, and my mind began to spin. I knew this would probably be the biggest story of my career.

The next few days, I did my best to put Google and Project Veritas to the back of my mind and tried to focus on the competition and enjoying my time in Korea, a country I had been wanting to travel to for years.

South Korea was an interesting country. What made the trip more interesting was that what spurred me to go there—to compete in a country western line dancing competition.

While I was there, I got to check one item off my bucket list: to visit the DMZ, or Demilitarized Zone, the stretch of land that separates North and South Korea. I've always found the hermit nation of North Korea to be a source of fascination for me. When I was an Army Officer, I read book after book about life in the country, written by those who had escaped.

I decided it would be fun to take a picture at the North Korean border wearing my Project Veritas hat and thought back on how it was ironic (and even a little sad) that I felt safer wearing that hat standing fifty feet away from North Korea than I did wearing it walking around downtown Austin.

I was a world away when the Google story was published, but twenty-four hours later, I landed at JFK and headed to the office.

After that, it was a whirlwind of activity. Jen Gennai, the Google executive with the Orwellian title, Head of Responsible Innovation, posted on Medium, trying to defend the damning words she had spoken about Google's plans for the 2020 election.

> In late May, I accepted an invitation to meet with a few people who claimed to be from "2 Step Tech Solutions." They said they wanted to chat to me about a mentoring program for young women of color in tech, an area I've long been passionate about. We went for dinner at a restaurant in the Mission, San Francisco.

Unfortunately, I now know that these people lied about their true identities, filmed me without my consent, selectively edited and spliced the video to distort my words and the actions of my employer, and published it widely online. I now know they belong to a group called Project Veritas, which has done this to numerous other people working in the tech and other sectors.

Why did they do this to me? It seems they found that I had spoken publicly at Google I/O on Ethics, and they wanted someone who would give them juicy soundbites about tech's alleged bias against conservatives. Over the course of a two-hour dinner, I guess they think I delivered.

Jen Gennai tried to downplay the importance of her role at Google. Don't let the Medium article fool you. She was one of the heads of Trust and Safety at Google and was now the Head of Responsible Innovation, which dealt with Google's artificial intelligence, aka machine learning programs such as the ML Fairness documents the Google insider Zach Voorhies had leaked to us.

Having heard the horror stories of James and other Project Veritas journalists being detained at customs when reentering the United States, I held my breath as I went through customs and immigration at JFK. Thankfully, nothing happened, but I realized I was making some extremely powerful enemies.

I had helped expose some of the most powerful corporations in the world and some of the most prominent politicians, and found glaring vulnerabilities in our electoral system, including potential voting by illegal aliens in Travis County, Texas, and double voting in New Hampshire and Florida, the latter of which even led to a felony conviction.

For the tech companies, I was at the very least a thorn in their side. Shortly after the video of Jen Gennai was released, Google fought back, taking the video down from YouTube after over a million views citing "privacy violations." They definitely suppressed the content because to this day, if you search "Project Veritas Google," the exposé, even in its reuploaded, edited format, doesn't come up.

In a US Senate hearing, Senator Ted Cruz asked another Google executive, "Are you familiar with the report that was released yesterday from Veritas that included a whistleblower from within Google and videos from a senior executive at Google, that included documents that are purportedly internal PowerPoint documents from Google?"

"Yes, I heard about that report in industry news."

"Have you seen the report?"

"No, I have not."

"So you didn't review the report to prepare for this hearing?"

"It's been a busy day, and I have a day job, which is digital well-being at Google, so I'm trying to keep this train on the tracks."

"Well, I'm sorry this hearing is impinging on your day job."

Cruz continued, "So a different individual, a whistleblower identified simply as an insider at Google with knowledge of the algorithm, is quoted on the same report as saying Google 'is bent on never letting somebody like Donald Trump come to power again.' Do you think it's Google's job to make sure 'somebody like Donald Trump never comes to power again'?"

Eventually, the Jen Gennai story led to James being invited to the White House for the Social Media Summit. President Trump personally recognized James and, by extension, everyone at Project Veritas.

Over the course of eighteen months, I had gone from being alone with my documents, unsure, afraid, and feeling like I had somehow failed because I hadn't accomplished enough with my life, to getting praise from the most powerful man on earth. Finally, my work, drive, and passion were making an impact.

All I had wanted to do from the time I was young was to make a difference in this world. I tried to do that by becoming an Army Officer but was never able to make it to the front lines of the fight. Once I was in a car accident and my career was cut short, I lost my identity. With all the crises that followed, I felt even more beat down by life.

Knowing that one of my best friends had his life taken from him gave me a reason to try again even though all the odds seemed stacked against me. Ascending to be someone better than the person I started out as was the best way to honor Matty's legacy.

Although I was having great success in my professional life, I would have left it all to have my daughter back. No matter how big of a story I broke, the pain of not having my child to raise never went away.

CHAPTER 24

Fighting Back

IN A DANCE STUDIO IN NEW HAMPSHIRE, MY HEART was breaking. I was on the phone with my daughter, Lexi, for her birthday. I reluctantly called Doug, knowing that any phone calls I had with my daughter would be like talking to someone in prison.

"We decided that we're going to try homeschool."

"Are you still doing Girl Scouts?"

"No."

No matter how many politicians I was able to expose, no matter what kind of corporate wrongdoing I was able to bring to light, the one thing that I never was able to get past mentally was how my daughter had been wrongfully taken from me and was now being raised by my father in the type of home where women are taught that being homemakers should be their ultimate purpose in life.

A home that when you're raped as a teenager, you're told to stop being a "drama queen."

A home that allowed hired help to take advantage of your brother, and when it gets brought up later on, dismiss his concerns and tell him he "liked it."

I ground my teeth together as I tried to practice basic dance steps in the mirror while on the phone with my daughter. She was now living in total isolation from the outside world, and I wouldn't stop fighting for her.

Using the money I had saved up, I got enough to pay my attorney another retainer to file a petition to modify, citing that there had been a significant change of circumstances since the previous round of hearings.

I found out that Doug had somehow convinced the state of Virginia to allow him to take in foster children, and now there were at least four additional children living in the home, including older boys. Knowing my own experience with sexual assault, this chilled me to the bone.

Lexi used to have dreams of becoming a Blue Angel pilot,

or a teacher, or a doctor, depending on what day you asked her. I knew that preteens start to become sulky and withdrawn, but my daughter seemed like a hollow shell of the bright ambitious girl whom I had raised.

Every once in a while, I would come home to another letter that had clearly been heavily influenced, if not flat-out dictated, by Doug. Letters telling me I should "repent" or to tell me to "stop with all this court stuff."

It was a fight and took a major emotional toll on me just to talk to Lexi on the phone; it was heartbreaking every time because I could feel her drifting further and further from me.

People tell me I'm strong for working as hard as I did and pushing through the pain of being separated from my daughter.

Usually, my response is that I wasn't strong naturally. I only became strong because my other option was to crumble and wither away, which would have proved all the horrible things Doug said about me to be true.

CHAPTER 25

The Pain of Uncertainty

"The arc of the universe is long, but it bends towards justice."

—MARTIN LUTHER KING JR.

JAMES WOULD FREQUENTLY REMIND ME OF THIS quote during the times I would get down about the situation with Lexi.

For a long time, the situation was something I compartmentalized and instead focused on work and dance. But in the fall as my next court date approached, I was a mess. Normally during a release week, I'd be pumped, and I'd be all dolled up at work.

That week, I rolled into work wearing a shirt with the

words "I'M A MESS" written on it in huge block lettering and black leggings with my hair in a ponytail and no makeup on. I just couldn't bring myself to be excited about anything. The story was huge, one of the biggest in Project Veritas history, and our CNN insider was directly inspired by me.

Cary Poarch is an amazing human being and a patriot. He and his family put so much on the line to record hundreds of hours of footage from within CNN, and I desperately wanted to celebrate, but real life was hitting me and hard.

The whistleblower program had come a long way since I had my first meetings with Ken in 2017. My situation was unique for a number of reasons, but although I felt proud watching the outpouring of public support, there was a part of me (the part with mounting legal bills and creditors calling routinely to remind me of all the things that still weren't paid off) that was a little frustrated.

When I blew the whistle, there was no GoFundMe set up on my behalf.

I didn't have a small staff of Project Veritas journalists there to be my emotional support in the days that followed.

I didn't even have someone checking in on me via text.

From the time I was fired from Facebook until I met with James in New York seven months later, I sat in silence, thinking Project Veritas had just abandoned me and left me to rot on my own.

Of course by now, I knew the truth of what had *actually* been going on at the time, but that didn't diminish the fact there was a month where my roommate and I knew that if something didn't happen, it would be the last month we could afford rent.

I did what I could to make money, such as donating plasma twice a week.

Even though that was all behind me now, the trauma still remained. As successful as I was, I constantly found myself being paranoid that what I was doing wasn't enough and that someday, I would wake up and it would all be gone and I'd be right back where I started.

First, I had to learn to trust myself again. Self-doubt becomes a self-fulfilling prophecy. I had to remind myself of how much I had accomplished, even before I ever became the Facebook whistleblower. I had to remind myself that I was a good mother. From afar, I knew the best way to continue doing that was to lead by example. Be strong, be brave, work hard, and when life inevitably knocks you down, get back up.

This was a mantra I had always lived by, going so far as having the Japanese proverb "Seven times fall down, eight times stand up" tattooed on the back of my leg.

In the first court hearing in 2018, when my daughter was ripped from me, there was no support from Project Veritas. When I sobbed so hard that snot ran down my face, I didn't have a place to turn. We hadn't released the story yet, so the public didn't know there was a Facebook whistleblower. How could they help me and spread word of my story when they didn't know my identity?

Financially, and even worse, emotionally and psychologically, I had been left alone. I would look at presentations and see each of the whistleblowers who came after me and hear about the speaking engagements they were giving, but my face remained in the shadows. I've never been one to seek attention or fame, but I always worried the public would perceive it as cowardice on my behalf, when the reality was that I had been so effective as an undercover journalist that the decision was made that it was more beneficial for me to remain in the dark and continue exposing the Big Tech companies, crooked politicians, and so forth.

The weekend before my court date, I was at a dance competition in Panama City, Florida. The week before, I had been at the Project Veritas office to celebrate the release of our CNN insider, but I found it hard to smile. Cary (the insider) had been inspired by me after hearing my story during James's speech at CPAC, and I should have been proud, thrilled, and excited.

The first day of the dance competition, I won in the open division in pro-am and got my highest scores of the season.

But on the second day, when I was competing in the line dance division, David chided me for not smiling during my first routine.

As the court date loomed, it was becoming increasingly impossible for me to hide all the pain and anguish I had covered up working and dancing for the past year. To be forcibly separated from my daughter and to know that she was in a horrific situation I was powerless to change challenged everything I believed about justice and in particular, my ability to make an impact.

How is it that I could affect elections and take on tech giants, but I was powerless to help the person who mattered the most? How could I go from being so terrified of dancing in public to someone who wasn't only entering dance competitions but was also winning awards for the very thing that used to be one of her biggest fears?

There were a lot of children competing in this competition in particular, and they brought so much joy to the room. At the same time, however, there was a part of my heart and my stomach that sank at not being able to share the joy I had found in my life with Lexi—to have her be part of the families I had found both in the dance community and at Project Veritas.

"Just give me a smile for two minutes?" David asked.

I finished my last dance and went straight from the dance floor to my hotel room, my eyes welling up with angry tears about how unfair all of it was.

It was Sunday, and with all my dance friends saying they would be sending prayers and positive vibes my way, I knew Wednesday (the day court was set for), it was time to go to war.

I emphasized how awful it was the first time I went to court to contrast it with my mental state going into the second hearing. Although I still felt generally miserable, because let's face it, family court is not a place anyone wants to be, this time, I wasn't alone.

Even though we had known each other for over a year and had built a strong foundation of trust, I was afraid to ask James if he would come to testify on my behalf. This wasn't his problem. He didn't create it, he didn't ask to be involved in it, and yet I knew his showing up would show the courts that I was fired from Facebook for being a corporate whistleblower, that I was in fact a stable person and a good employee, and I was a strong and brave person—not the mental headcase Doug had painted me out to be.

Admittedly, the petty part of me also wanted to see the look on Doug's when he saw James O'Keefe, the person he said would never know who I was, right there in court with me.

I asked James, and he said yes. He actually cleared his schedule and canceled another engagement that was booked that day so he could make the court date.

Prior to my working at Project Veritas, I made a point to research James as much as I could. A profile in Politico titled "James O'Keefe Can't Get No Respect" said of him:

> During my time with O'Keefe and his fresh-faced posse, I never once witnessed any of them challenge him. O'Keefe is known to be brutal on his employees; they are, by and large, a collection of young yes-men.

I will say that after one year of working for James O'Keefe, even though he has high expectations for his employees, for sure, he is the best boss I've ever had. That includes my time in the Army, Facebook, and other organizations. James is the perfect example of not asking your subordinates anything you would be unwilling to do yourself. This book is not a Project Veritas tell-all, but I will say there were instances where I challenged James on something, and even though he had the ultimate, final say (he is the boss after all), I don't think anyone at the company would have described me as a yes-man.

The fact that James was willing to travel to the middle-of-nowhere Virginia to help me get my daughter back is something I will never forget, and it is a debt I will never find a way to properly repay.

CHAPTER 26

Fear and Loathing in Farmville

I COULD FEEL THE RAGE STARTING TO BUILD AS I drove my rental car from DC to Farmville, Virginia. My second court hearing was upon me, and my mood would switch from being confident and self-assured to feeling like a tiny, scared child again.

The day before court, the opposing counsel sent over a ridiculous settlement offer. Four weeks of visitation, supervised by Doug—*at his house*. I was also required to talk to his hired help, Beth Cook, the same therapist who had high-fived him outside of the courtroom.

I picked up James in Raleigh, and we made the drive to Farmville. Ever the executive, he spent most of the drive on staff calls. As we drove into areas so rural that there was no cell phone reception, I noticed him looking around. He must have noticed the death grip I had on the steering wheel, knowing what lay ahead of me.

I told James my expectations for the hearing were low, given how I was treated by the Farmville family court the first time around. We did discuss what would happen if I were to get custody back. I told him if that were to happen, there was no way I'd be able to continue to go undercover.

As an undercover journalist, I spent 95 percent of my time on the road. My animals barely remembered me when I came home. Being a single parent, there was no way around it. James nodded gravely. If I were to win in court, it would mean he would lose a journalist who had been successful in the field.

To have a justice complex is to be compelled to do the right thing, even when it is in direct opposition with what is in your self-interest.

When we walked up to the courthouse, there was a group of prisoners in orange jumpsuits being led out in shackles. James looked at me, his eyes asking if I were serious this was where we were supposed to be.

"It's kind of a one-stop-shop courthouse." I laughed.

We waited in the hallway outside of the courtroom where my mom and her husband were waiting, along with my attorney. My mom had never met James, and this was certainly a bit of an awkward situation for everyone involved, given that we were all there to testify in my custody case, and for James, for a child he had never met.

I wanted my mom to meet James, who had been such a driving force in helping me get my fire back. And I wanted James to meet my mom, especially after sharing stories about my childhood growing up with a tiger mom and being forced to play the piano for hours a day. This awkward courtroom lobby meet-and-greet, however, was not what I had envisioned.

The way Farmville family court works is everyone waits in a main courtroom that looks like most other courtrooms in the country. However, the actual hearing itself is held in a tiny room off to the side, which, in retrospect, is somewhat indicative of how family court conducts itself—it looks like a regular court, but the way in which it behaves is anything but.

Doug arrived with his wife. I noticed it seemed that he had aged at least ten years since the last hearing. He looked tired and old. He was always short of stature, but his presence had been large and intimidating. That's how he ruled his household after all. But now, he looked small.

I would say pitiful, but he is such a horrible human being that I felt no pity for him. I could tell there was a look of surprise on his face when he saw James there with me, which was exactly what I wanted. I had the truth on my side, and I had a "bigger fish" than Doug ever could be to vouch for me. James, at 6'1", towered over Doug at 5'3", which gave a visual representation to the energy in the room. In contrast, I did my best to display the inner confidence that successfully taking on politicians and Big Tech felt on the outside. I was dazzling. I mean that literally. But that's partially because of an explosion of glitter that happened in my makeup bag from a dance competition.

My ex-husband, Lexi's father Jason, was there as well. He, too, looked old. With a scraggly goatee and graying hair, he looked more like a homeless person and nothing like the soldier I married when I was nineteen.

"*That's* your ex-husband?" James said to me with more than a little bit of judgment in his voice.

"I was nineteen," I replied, embarrassed.

Between having my mother there, James, and an attorney, I felt confident and mentally prepared for the hearing. Although I recognized I probably wasn't going to walk away with full custody, I felt confident that I was at least going to leave with more than I had, which was nothing.

When it was our turn to be called to the small side room, they let in Doug and his wife, Jason, even though he was not named in the case, and Jason's parents who had accompanied him to court.

When I walked in, they let me and my lawyer in, but said my mom, her husband, and James would have to wait outside. They didn't give me a reason, and I had been coached by my attorney that my best bet was to appear compliant, even though every instinct I had was telling me to fight. After spending a year around corruption, I could sense when something was off. They swore everyone in at once and I sat down, irritated.

The judge said first the court would determine if there had been a "significant" change of circumstance, and once that was determined, they would hear the merits of the hearing.

I was called to the stand and asked the following:

Where I worked (Project Veritas).

How long I had worked there (a year).

How much my salary was (enough to not be on food stamps or for it to be a concern for the court).

If I had any medical conditions, physical or mental (insomnia and anxiety).

Why I was coming to court (to restore my parental rights).

When Doug's attorney cross-examined me, they asked if I was "still hearing voices" because I felt that Matty would talk to me following his murder. Doug also knew that whenever I went to DC, I would stop by Arlington National Cemetery to update Matty on whatever was going on in my life.

They also attacked me for not going to Doug's house to see my child. I told them I did not want to spend time with my abuser.

When I said the word *abuser*, I looked Doug straight in the eye. For the first time, I wasn't afraid to call him by what he was. The things I endured growing up with him as my father were in fact a form of emotional abuse. What I thought was a close relationship was in fact a way for Doug to keep me dependent on him, and it isolated and ruined my relationships with others. Nothing spoke more to this than when I told my father about being raped and he told me to "stop being such a drama queen."

My attorney questioned Doug and established that:

1. Lexi had been pulled out of the private school she had

been attending, which was used at the previous hearing as a reason to keep her with Doug, and was being homeschooled.

2. Despite Doug promising that he would never take in foster children so long as Lexi was living in the house, there were now four foster children living in the house, including older boys.

3. The past three attempts I made to see my daughter had been denied by Doug.

Last, my attorney called in James, and we were told to keep the questions strictly to the basic details of my employment. Once a reasonable change of circumstances had been established, he could be called again to testify further on my character, my state of mind, and so forth.

They asked him his name, his job title, and how long I had been working for him. That was it. That's all they'd let him say. They asked him to leave the room again.

The fact that I was no longer impoverished combined with all the things that had happened with Lexi, the idea of not getting through that first part of the hearing never even crossed my mind. If that did not constitute a "significant change of circumstance," what did?

They turned to Jimmy Bell, the guardian ad litem, to ask his thoughts. Despite my attorney's assurances that

Jimmy was a good man and a truly neutral third party, I never trusted him. He was a short man with a weasel-like appearance, a speech impediment, and a limp.

Ever the journalist, I found out he had been arrested the year prior for a DUI, and along with personal injury, DUI defense happened to be one of Doug's areas of law practice. Additionally, I saw he was no longer listed as a guardian ad litem on the court's website.

This was the man who had, at one point, yelled at me on the phone that I should spend time with my abuser and just reconcile and be a happy family.

My faith in him was low, but surely, he couldn't deny that circumstances were vastly different in 2019 than they were in 2018.

Right?

"It's my opinion that there has not been a significant change of circumstance."

When he told the judge that he felt that there had been no significant change of circumstance, it took every ounce of my self-control to not shout out in the courtroom. The judges in this small town (I had a different one this time) had always just gone with whatever Jimmy said, which is how I was told that things worked in this town of 7,800 people.

When the judge said we were not going to proceed with the hearing any further, I immediately stood up.

"We *will* be appealing."

I was breaking inside, but I knew I was in the presence of the enemy, so I refused to show any weakness.

James and I went back to the rental car and said he would get an Uber to get to the Richmond airport. I snorted and said, "There's no Uber service out here." He asked if I was going to try and see my daughter while I was in town. I said yes but that I had been through this several times before. Every time I asked Doug if I could see Lexi, there was always some excuse as to why I couldn't despite traveling thousands of miles.

"We have plans," he said this time.

"See? Told you," I said to James who shook his head. "Let's get out of this shithole," I said, pulling out of town.

Having my boss there kept me from breaking down in the car. I was enraged. I felt impotent. How could I take on some of the biggest corporations the world has ever seen and get defeated in this corrupt, small-town court?

It was time to dig back into work, though admittedly that was getting harder to do since not only was I separated from my daughter, but she was in a situation I found to be genuinely dangerous.

CHAPTER 27

Iowa

MAGGIE

I HAD BEEN WORKING IN AND OUT OF IOWA throughout the Democratic primaries. I had bounced around from campaign to campaign, feeling them out to figure out where I thought there was a story.

I seemed to be most at home with the Bernie Sanders campaign since they were the same sorts of people I had dealt with in the past, both with the Austin DSA as well as the Beto campaign.

A lot of the Beto staffers in the Texas senate race were Bernie Bros who turned on Beto when he tried to take a more moderate tone in the arguably purple state of Texas. So it was no surprise that once it came time for the presidential run, all of Beto's support suddenly evaporated. Bernie was always their guy; Beto was just someone they thought could start to turn Texas blue.

I was surprised at how quickly I became friends with the Bernie staffers, although I guess I shouldn't be, considering this had been my job for over a year, and in some ways, they reminded me of friends from college or back home.

If I were to give any advice to anyone considering a career in undercover journalism, this is a perfect example of why you *don't* go in with an agenda. Do your research, see if there are any signs of something that may be a lead, of course; but if the story takes another turn, go with it.

One of the Bernie staffers I befriended was a woman named Maggie. She had worked on Beto's senate campaign, so we quickly bonded over being from Texas. She was a former healthcare worker who was struggling to make ends meet. She was also a mother with a daughter similar in age to me.

I enjoyed most of the conversations I had with Maggie. Even though I 100 percent disagreed with her politics, I didn't think of her as a bad-intentioned person. In fact, I related to her in a lot of ways. After the Beto campaign had ended, she continued to struggle. She got a job with the Bernie campaign, but they didn't tell her they wouldn't have housing for her and her children.

One time over lunch, a storm suddenly came in. Maggie immediately got on the phone, worried her husband wouldn't be able to put up the tent so that things didn't get wet.

I assumed she meant some of the tents the staffers would put up at campaign events, so I was confused as to why her husband, who didn't work on the campaign, needed to do it.

She told me they had been camping since they got there, but I thought she meant maybe just sleeping on a floor until her furniture arrived. No, she meant it literally. She, her husband, her children, and her pets had been living out of her minivan and in tents since they arrived in Iowa, at least a month prior.

I'm sure the difference was subtle enough that she didn't notice, but in that moment, I dropped whatever cover I had and offered to do whatever I could to help her out. I asked if she needed help moving things indoors, and I gave her a ride back to the campaign office, since her husband needed their one vehicle to move their belongings out of the rain. Maggie said her husband had it covered but thanked me for offering.

The rain was coming down so hard that we both screamed as we ran to where my car was parked. I was soaked, and

I worried at some point, my camera equipment would malfunction or that I'd be electrocuted.

Maggie graciously offered to give me one of the "Bernie for Iowa" shirts the campaign had in storage since I was soaked to the bone. I gladly took it. I didn't want Maggie and her family to be homeless out in a storm, so without thinking, I offered to help her get a hotel room for the night.

When you are guided by principles of justice and truth telling, there are times that even though on the surface it may seem an odd thing to do, you go ahead and do the right thing. And a Project Veritas journalist trying to help an unwitting Bernie Sanders staffer and her family have a dry comfortable place to sleep for the night was the right thing to do.

I offered without asking Elton but later was told I did the right thing. Everyone in the company agreed I made the right call.

In fact, I originally found the whole situation so hypocritical and appalling that I thought that was the story. Maggie and I became closer after she disclosed her situation with me, and I would serve as a sounding board and someone she could talk to about work. I learned about how poorly the Bernie campaign treated its staff. For a campaign that made such a big show of "We're unionized! We care about workers!" its actions were completely hypocritical.

The idea of a Project Veritas union is laughable, but I can say that there is a 0 percent chance the company would ever put an employee in a position like that.

It wasn't just Maggie. It turned out that within the campaign's senior staff, there were other union-busting activities going on. I continued to remain curious and listen, thinking that my story would expose the massive hypocrisy of Bernie Sanders since Maggie had made her situation very clear to the senior staff member who then did nothing to step in and help her.

I didn't feel bad at all during this time because the campaign had been treating her poorly and I felt no guilt about exposing them for it.

Remember, though, how I said that you don't know where a story is going to go?

Then one day, at a campaign volunteer training, I met Kyle Jurek.

CHAPTER 28

Iowa

KYLE

I THOUGHT I ALREADY HAD MY BERNIE SANDERS story, so when another field organizer, Kyle, asked me to get coffee with him, I kind of sighed and thought, *Oh yay, more paperwork for me to do*. Like any journalist, undercover or otherwise, every meeting we had needed to have notes and reports sent back to the office.

But I agreed. When I initially met him at the campaign office, he didn't come off as particularly crazy or anything. I decided to meet with him in order to cast as wide a net as possible (because that was my job), but my expectations for the meeting were low.

My journalist radar shot up the second he opened up his

laptop and I saw a huge sticker that read "ANTIFA" across the top. I had met with radicals in the Bernie campaign, but a lot of them were guarded about it because they knew they had to appeal to the crowd in Iowa.

Kyle started talking about how he and another organizer wanted to recruit me for a "direct action" team. This team was going to go out, not wearing official Bernie campaign merch, of course, and participate in more extreme forms of demonstration than what would be considered acceptable by an actual political campaign.

Apparently, one of the things they wanted to start with was finding where the small ICE presence was in Des Moines so they could "harass" ICE agents. The idea was to have a team of volunteers, organized and directed by the Bernie campaign, act as a more radical wing of the campaign to help further the overall progressive cause.

Kyle was not like Maggie. He was in his late thirties, had no kids, was never married, and had no significant career accomplishments to speak of. He, like most of the other Bernie staffers, were potheads, and Kyle talked about drinking and partying, which in contrast to me, in my early thirties, I felt I had already outgrown.

His demeanor and the way he carried himself also told me that instead of being a good-hearted person whom I disagreed with on policy, he was someone interested in altercations, even violent ones, and felt that those on the political right (and even liberals) needed to get on board with his cause or face drastic repercussions.

As a woman, I can instinctually tell when a man is interested in me, and Kyle was interested in the woman I was pretending to be. I was wearing a fake wedding ring and talked about my husband who was overseas, but he still invited me to go have drinks with him a couple of days later.

I talked with Elton and the team at HQ, and this was the first time in my entire undercover career that someone I interacted with gave me a bad feeling. You could attribute it to my years of military training or to being a woman and just knowing when a guy is a creep, but Kyle gave off that vibe.

Until I could get backup, I stuck to hanging out with Kyle at the campaign office. One time, he got particularly angry and actually began yelling and cursing at a voter while phone banking who questioned Bernie Sanders's socialist policies. Having phone banked for numerous campaigns, I can tell you that people are sometimes flat-out rude to you on the phone. If you're lucky and they don't want to talk, they'll just hang up on you. Phone banking for Bernie Sanders, I definitely had my share of angry Trump supporters answer my calls. I would always laugh in my head thinking, *Oh, if only you knew.*

The man Kyle was talking to was a social studies teacher, and Kyle began to insult the man saying how he was uneducated. I couldn't believe how unprofessional he was. It was phone banking. I had always been taught that if someone was clearly not going to change their mind on the topic, politely thank them for their time and wish them a good evening.

Kyle was heated and went outside to smoke. I didn't smoke, so it was a little awkward, but I knew that this would be a good time to talk to him about the radical vision he and the other Bernie staffers had for the world.

I asked him about the call even though I had already heard it since he was shouting loudly in the office. He vented about it, and then the subject turned to how many actual communists and Marxists supported Bernie Sanders.

Me: I know we've got the communists and the Marxists on our side.

Kyle: Yeah, and I'm one of them.

He said it so casually as he waved his hand and smoked a

cigarette. I asked what he would label himself politically. He said he was an anarcho-communist.

I never portrayed myself as someone uneducated on politics, but Kyle then felt the need to, in probably the only time I ever felt someone was trying to mansplain something to me, what the political compass looks like and where he fell on it.

Then he said something I will never forget: "If you don't love me at my most communist, you don't deserve me at my most anarchist."

Sometimes when someone says something, you just *know* it will end up in the final release (and it did). *The_Donald subreddit would have a field day*, I thought to myself.

Thankfully, they sent Ryan, a fellow military veteran, to accompany me from now on. He was going to play my brother-in-law. Having Ryan there was a welcome relief since not only did he add a sense of security, but it meant that at the end of the day, I could go have dinner with a coworker and let down the pretenses of the day, not just hope that Elton needed an update on how things were going to get that release.

Kyle invited me to a blues festival at a local club, and I told him I was bringing Ryan with me. I don't smoke, but

I knew Kyle did, and so instinctively I told Ryan to stop by a smoke shop so I could buy a vape pen and would have an excuse to go outside the noisy club to talk.

We went to the club, and there were several Bernie staffers there. Eventually, everyone moved out to the back to chill and talk. I danced with one of the staffers, and in general, we had a good time. One of the staffers, Jessica, came up with a shirt that said "Bernie Is My Comrade," which was enough for me to try and be sure I got a shot of it, but then I had her list off the other historical figures who were pictured alongside the octogenarian "democratic socialist." They included people such as Lenin, Stalin, and Mao. The staffers drank, smoked, laughed, and sang the praises of those communist dictators and others, such as Fidel Castro. They talked about getting the "Bernie Is My Comrade" images on stickers to give out at the office.

The field office they worked in covered the greater Des Moines area, by far the most populous area of Iowa. This wasn't one, two, or three radicals working in the office; these were the beliefs of the *whole* office, including Justin, who had just been promoted to being in charge of it.

In fact, the only one who didn't espouse these extreme views was Maggie, whom I heard the other staffers say negative things about over the course of the evening.

Already, Ryan and I knew the content we had would be shocking for most voters to hear. It was a lot, even for me, someone who had been in the campaigns of just about every Democrat who was running for president in 2020. The Bernie people were different. They didn't just want to win an election—they wanted to destroy America as we knew it.

It was already around 1:00 a.m. when Ryan and I began to walk back to the car, feeling accomplished, and Kyle chased us down in the street. Ryan and I were both tired, but Kyle wanted the three of us to grab pizza.

We both sighed before turning around and smiling. Even though we were exhausted, the mission always came first, so off we went to get pizza.

At this point, Kyle fully trusted Ryan and me. Feeling comfortable expressing his true feelings, he talked about himself and the other Bernie campaign radicals who wanted to put Trump supporters into "reeducation camps" and sing the praises of the Soviet gulags. I practically couldn't believe what I was hearing. He even talked about how liberals were at odds with the progressives, and he believed they could either stand aside and allow "the revolution" to happen or be lined up and shot. Knowing that both Ryan and I had a military background, he tried to use our experiences to justify the killing of anyone who would stand in the way of the revolution.

Kyle also wanted Ryan and me to take a road trip with him to Colorado, where he talked about us all going into the woods and drugs together, including hallucinogenic mushrooms, and then bringing a bunch of marijuana back to Iowa for the other Bernie staffers since his stash was running low and he was having issues finding drugs in Des Moines.

We were up with Kyle until probably 3:00 a.m. that day. Ryan and I got into our rental, satisfied we had found our story but also in disbelief at how open and brazen Kyle was talking about these things.

On the way back to the hotel, a cop pulled us over.

"What are you both doing out so late?"

"We're journalists."

"Oh, really?"

"Yeah."

"What are you covering?"

"Fighting communism."

"In Des Moines?"

"Yup."

And he let us on our way.

The next day, we both slept in before meeting in the outside lounge area of our hotel. I lay down on one of the benches, still feeling sick and my voice hoarse from all the nicotine I had taken in while chain-smoking the night prior.

Both being prior military, we discussed how someone like Kyle was the type of person who once the story was published, could go postal. Like I said, the guy was a loser, and the Bernie campaign and the revolution were all that he had.

We also theorized that if the Des Moines office was 90 percent radicals who were ready for a violent revolution, that might not be an anomaly in the Bernie campaign and suggested that other campaign offices were likely staffed with people similar to Kyle.

We weren't wrong.

CHAPTER 29

Tech Tries to Play Nice

ONE DAY AT WORK, I WAS TOLD THAT FACEBOOK had invited Project Veritas to be part of an ongoing set of meetings the company was having with different conservative groups. Earlier in the year, Mark Zuckerberg had dinner with Donald Trump, and it was clear that he was trying to make nice so the administration wouldn't go forward with threats to make changes that would either regulate Big Tech or alter Section 230 of the Communications Decency Act, which shields companies like Facebook from liability for content posted on their platform.

James was busy and couldn't attend, but I was in the office when he smiled at me and said, "What if we send *you*?"

The email said the format of the meeting would be a roundtable discussion and would include groups like Veritas and other conservatives, and a Facebook vice-president would "have a dialogue" with them.

"What if you just asked them why you were fired?"

I had provided indisputable evidence of bias—the company hadn't denied that any of the documents I submitted were true or accurate—yet Facebook was adamant it had no political bias. It was ridiculous.

So Brian and I attend the event for Project Veritas. We gave Facebook my real name, and the tech giant seemed happy that we wanted to participate in their "fruitful discussion."

I traveled to DC, mentally preparing to confront the Facebook talking head. I, a lowly, hourly contractor, asking a pointed and direct question to an executive, who probably made more money in a month than all my assets combined.

"Cassandra Spencer has been banned from Facebook premises," an email said the day before we were supposed to meet with the company.

I laughed and shook my head. I am certainly not any sort

of security risk to Facebook. These meetings with conservatives were nothing but a charade. They didn't, and still don't, want to be asked the hard questions, especially not by those who have worked at the company, know the corporate culture, and know what goes on behind the curtain.

A trillion-dollar corporation was afraid of me. I really had made an impact.

CHAPTER 30

The Iron Price

I HAVE ALWAYS BEEN AN OBSESSIVE *GAME OF Thrones* fan. In both the books and the show, there is a family of pirates (essentially) who pride themselves on not paying for the things they acquired with gold, but instead when they take them by force, or as the series puts it, "paying the iron price."

I was paying the iron price for the success I had achieved over the past year and a half.

I spent so much time flying around the country working on various stories for Project Veritas that by the time the holidays rolled around, I was extremely physically ill. The sinus infections I had been ignoring from the constant air travel had turned into pneumonia, and I was emotionally exhausted from the court battle I had been fighting for my daughter. On top of it, I was trying to prepare to go to Worlds for the first time to compete in dance.

On December 22, I was home in Texas on my way to the dance studio to rehearse when a car ran a stop sign and collided with my vehicle. I was knocked unconscious very briefly, and my memory of what happened is still spotty, but I do remember being unable to open my car door and getting help from a homeless man. I was pissed because Worlds was a week away and I had been training all year for it. Car accident or not, I wasn't about to let all that blood, sweat, tears, and money be for nothing.

I had a concussion, and my knee and shoulder were injured and would require physical therapy. Against medical advice, I went to Worlds in Nashville, and I remember between two heats of polka placing my head against a metal post because the whole room wouldn't stop spinning. David had to remind me to line up to get out on the floor. In the video of the event, you can see him trying to bounce up and down to remind me to smile, even though I felt like I was about to vomit.

One of the reasons I was so hell bent on doing Worlds, even after the injury, was because my brother Jeremy and his family were going to be there. It was the first time seeing him and his kids in a couple of years. It felt so good to have my brother there; he's the only person who can fully understand the hell of having Doug Spencer as a father. Jeremy, despite being a lifelong Democrat, was proud of me for the work I had done at Veritas. He knew his sister was someone who always wanted to do the right thing, regardless of the consequences. We both took refuge in how much better our lives had become once we finally cut out the cancer that was our "father." My brother saw how passionate I was about everything I did in life, whether it be journalism or dance.

"What are you going to do if and when you get Lexi back full time?" he asked me at one point.

"I'm not sure," I answered.

All things come to an end, and at the beginning of 2020, the expiration date for my time as an undercover journalist had come. I was physically and mentally drained and needed to take some time to focus on myself and my family and not be so entrenched in work. I had set out to make an impact on the world, and I did. Project Veritas now has a thriving insider program and has become the go-to place for Big Tech and media whistleblowers to tell the truth about the things going on in their respective institutions. Always a mom, I look at each story that comes out with a somewhat matronly pride, and I'm glad I had the experiences I did.

As the COVID pandemic set in, I was still trying to find my

way post-Veritas. At first, I wanted to pursue my dance passion as a new career, but as that industry was being decimated, I knew that that wasn't going to happen.

I watched as people around me struggled. I watched as cities began to burn in civil unrest, just as how Kyle had described back in Iowa. I watched Big Tech clamping down on conservative thought more and more. There was so much injustice still going on in the world, which made me wonder, I had made an impact, but was I supposed to keep fighting?

During my time at Veritas, I worked hard to reduce my digital footprint to almost nothing. I didn't want to be known. I had never been particularly comfortable with attention. Anytime James would congratulate me in front of my colleagues, I would turn bright red and just get quiet. I didn't do what I did for fame or recognition, and my credit cards certainly reflected that I didn't do it to get rich.

I did it because it was the right thing to do.

And even though I was happy with the idea of living a quiet life in Texas, there was still that voice inside of me that said I wasn't done, that my fight wasn't over. And in part, that's why I wrote this book—to tell my story in hopes that maybe it would inspire other insiders.

Or better yet, to reach a young person who maybe feels like their life doesn't matter and to show them instead that no matter how many times life knocks you down, it's never too late to get back up and make your impact.

Afterword

IT IS HARD FOR ME TO GIVE AN UPDATE ON WHERE my life is now because like the rest of the world, 2020 has been a year of absolute insanity. Between the time of this writing and when you are reading it, everything could have changed.

After Veritas, I started another job in conservative media that would have allowed me to have my daughter live with me since it did not require extensive travel. The battle for her began to take over more of my life. While working at my new job, I continued to pursue dancing competitively on a part-time basis. I thought maybe one day, another opportunity to do it full time and live a quiet life with my daughter would arise, and I would leave behind the world of politics completely.

Then, when the COVID pandemic hit, I lost my job because I had been doing field production work. With the country completely locked down, there was no longer a "field" for me to produce in. It was a frustrating situation for all involved.

Like millions of other people across our nation, I found myself once again unemployed. Considering that nearly everyone else around me also lost their jobs (when the dance studio was forced to close, all the instructors were laid off), I took solace that this was not a personal failure on my part.

Without being able to travel, though, I could not see Lexi, and all the hearings were postponed.

Even though it is no one's fault this happened, Lexi being further under Doug's thumb has alienated her to levels I never thought possible. After receiving numerous letters and calls telling me how I needed to repent, that I was going to hell, and that if I didn't, bad things would happen to me, I realized Lexi had been brainwashed to the point where a specialist would need to be brought in or enough time would need to pass for her to be old enough to have independence from Doug.

This book was, for a long time, an idea that I had merely toyed around with. The driving desire to write it was to have a physical manifestation of this period of time in my life so that when my daughter eventually became curious and had questions about what and who her mother was, she would know exactly what was going through my head at the time. With COVID, I suddenly had an abundance of time, so I began to write.

What was an idea became a reality, when my identity was somehow leaked to the media in the summer of 2020. *The New Republic*, a once-respected *New Yorker*-type publication but has since fallen from grace and is now more of a crappy blog à la *Gawker* (RIP) or *The Daily Beast*, ran a hit piece that included a lot of ridiculous personal information, including photos of me at an anime convention. Real newsworthy stuff.

The reporters who wrote it were not content with merely publishing the hit piece, however. They continued to harass and stalk me for at least a month after publication. I mostly ignored them and focused my efforts on figuring out what to do next with my life, when inadvertently, they made that path clear for me.

I had moved from Round Rock to another suburb in the general Austin metro area, when one day, I had a friend over.

Okay, I'll be honest, it was a Tinder date. I've been single for years and there's a pandemic.

I didn't tell this guy about my previous employment at Project Veritas because, well, I didn't feel the need to until we had been on several dates. He had never heard of it, which isn't entirely uncommon for people who aren't super political.

One day, he came over to a place I was sharing with an old Army buddy, and when he left, he said, "I think I need to find somewhere else to park next time I come to your house."

"Why?" I asked. "There is ample street parking here."

"Oh, I don't know. Someone was giving me a dirty look."

I instantly began to feel paranoid after the media harassment that had already occurred but told myself to calm down. It was probably nothing.

My initial instinct was right. Later that week, the guy I was dating informed me that some reporters (the same who had written the previous hit piece) had contacted him via Twitter and sent him surveillance photographs of me walking him out of the house.

A hard line had been crossed for me. This was the first person I had dated in several years. He had absolutely nothing to do with anything I had done at Project Veritas.

So I went public. I did not ask for permission. I had not worked at Project Veritas for months, but these media people were not leaving me alone. With the help of some of the other whistleblowers and some of the conservative media who knew of my past work, I began to tell my own story. My way.

I still maintain a good relationship with my past employer and will always stand by the journalism that Project Veritas does. Having worked there, I *know* how diligent they are before releasing anything.

James O'Keefe will always be someone I am eternally grateful for. Obvious professional dealings aside, he was willing to show up at a Farmville family court to testify on my behalf. That means more to me than any job or amount of money ever will.

But the time for me to step out from the shadows and be Cassandra has come. The recent world events have underscored the importance of calling out Big Tech censorship and the dangers of the far left. So now instead of a hidden camera, I use my voice to tell my story of being both an insider and a journalist.

I have developed a deep emotional connection to Texas, specifically Central Texas where I live. With more tech companies moving to Austin, I use my voice to encourage others to blow the whistle and point them in the direction of Project Veritas. This is also my home now, where I have people who love and care about me, and now that I'm not on the road so much, I try to give back to the community that has stood by me through a media firestorm I did not ask for.

Because of my renewed commitment to fighting for freedom, transparency, and justice, I plan on seeking elected office. In addition to Big Tech reforms and fighting the threat of communism, I want to be an outspoken advocate for reforming the broken and corrupt family court system that somehow has my child, who has two living parents, neither of whom are unfit, living in what is clearly an extremist situation under Doug.

Whether it be through elected office or not, one thing is for certain: I will make sure my voice is one that continues to make a positive impact on this world.

You can learn more about my current advocacy work, upcoming campaign (maybe), or ask questions about my story by visiting my website cassandraspencertx.com, or by following me on any of the major social media platforms (assuming I haven't joined the ranks of the banned by the time of publication).

Acknowledgments

FIRST, I WOULD LIKE TO THANK THE FAMILY THAT has stuck with me through this journey. That includes my mother and her husband, my brother and his family, and the small amount of family I have in Austin.

Second, I would like to thank James O'Keefe. Thank you for believing me and for always having my back. You were there for me in some of my darkest hours and that is something I will never, ever forget.

This story would also be nothing without the rest of the team at Project Veritas. From my supervisor "Elton," whom I've probably cried to more than my fair share of times, to the production team and other office staff— you've been nothing but incredible, and it was a pleasure to work with such an amazing team. A special thanks to

"Brienne," who has become one of my best friends. I miss our hotel sleepovers, and I know that I've found a lifelong friend in you.

Thank you to David Miller, who helped me rediscover my love of the performing arts and stuck with me even when I would book lessons with less than twenty-four hours' notice since I never knew when I was coming home, and half the time, I would have just gotten off a plane. You've been an amazing coach, therapist, and friend. You never gave up on me or let me give up on myself. Getting to know you and your family has been a true blessing in my life here. Thank you to Karen Miller for being a wonderful friend and for becoming the closest thing I have to family in Texas.

Additionally, thank you to each and every one of the dance instructors and coaches I've learned from during this journey. This is not a book about dance, but to say that it was not a source of comfort and strength during this time would be dishonest. I apologize to all the dancers I gave a fake name to, but, well, now you know why.

Thank you, Mariann Pino, for being like a sister to me and for always accepting me just the way I am.

To my roommate, Casey, thank you for always being sure I had a safe home to come back to and for putting up with the craziness you never signed up for but that came simply from living with me.

Christopher Biddie, my bff4l4realz, thank you for always being there for me in a way that only an Army friend can be—by relentlessly making fun of me anytime I tried to actually be serious about anything.

Jessica, one of my best friends since high school, you have been with me through every step of this journey, from the first time I met James through now. Thank you for always opening your home to me and for being an amazing friend.

And to all my friends back home who've known me since childhood (David, Cassie, and Claire). Thank you for always being supportive, for never forgetting the real me, and for not believing the caricature created by the media.

About the Author

CASSANDRA SPENCER is a former US Army Public Affairs Officer turned Facebook insider turned Project Veritas undercover journalist. Her work has generated millions of views on social media, prompted investigations at the local, state, and federal levels, and in one instance, even led to a felony conviction. She describes herself as having a justice complex from a young age and has devoted her life to fighting for what she believes in, both personally and professionally.